THE LIGHT OF THE WORLD

THE LIGHT

by Jaroslav Pelikan **OF**

THE WORLD

A Basic Image in Early Christian Thought

HARPER & BROTHERS, PUBLISHERS, NEW YORK

To
O. P. Kretzmann,
President, Valparaiso University

The James A. Gray Fund was established at the Divinity School of Duke University in 1946 as a part of the Methodist College Advance of the North Carolina Conference of the Methodist Church. The purpose of the fund, in the words of the donor, is to expand and maintain the educational services of the Duke Divinity School in "behalf of the North Carolina churches and pastors, particularly rural churches and pastors."

The present volume represents the eleventh series of the Gray Lectures, delivered in 1960.

Contents

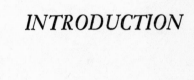

INTRODUCTION

"IN THY LIGHT DO WE SEE LIGHT": these words from Psalm 36:9 sound one of the most intriguing themes in the entire history of religion. The New Testament echoes this same theme when it declares that "God is light" (1 John 1:5). Readers of the Bible, both Jewish and Christian, have always recognized that there are parallels between this biblical theme and the worship of light in various pagan religions. Thus Martin Luther noted that the Babylonians

> . . . worshiped God under the title of light, which is the best figure or representation of the Divine Majesty; the Holy Scriptures themselves call God "light."[1]

And in its conflicts with Gnosticism early Christianity saw both the similarities and the differences between the dualistic doctrines of the Gnostics about light and darkness and the biblical understanding of God in Christ as the true light who dispels darkness.[2]

Yet it has not been until our own century that the depth and power of this imagery in the history of Near Eastern religion—and therefore the significance of this imagery for the interpretation of the Christian faith—have occupied the attention of scholarly research. Exactly fifty years ago James Breasted developed his assessment of the role played by the images of the sun and the Nile in the evolution of Egyptian religion, culminating in the "solar monotheism" of Ikhnaton.[3] Subsequent revisions of Breasted's theories do not reduce the importance of his work. At almost the same time as Breasted, the eminent patrologist and historian of religion, Franz Joseph Dölger, was publishing the first of his many monographs on the "sun of righteousness" and related images in early Christianity and in its pagan milieu.[4] The scholarly study of Hellenistic Judaism, which has also flourished during the twentieth century, has demonstrated how powerful the imagery of sun and light was in the thought and language of Philo.[5] This imagery helped to shape yet another constituent element of the world of early Christianity, the mystery religions. In the cult of the *Magna Mater*, for example, the *Hilaria* commemorated the resurrection of the god Attis on March 25, the day when the nights became shorter than the days.[6] Rudolf Bultmann has traced the transformation of the symbol of light as it passed from Greek to Hellenistic culture.[7] All this research makes it possible for present-day historians of religion to begin to draw certain conclusions about the provenance and range of "solar hierophanies." One historian has even been prompted to suggest this striking generalization:

> It is really only in Egypt, Asia and in primitive Europe that what we call sun-worship ever attained sufficient popularity to become at any time, as in Egypt for instance, really dominant. If you consider that, on the other side of the Atlantic, the solar religion was developed only in Peru and Mexico, only, that is, among the two "civilized" peoples of America, the only two who attained any level of real political organization, then you cannot help discerning a certain connection between the predominance of sun religions and what I may call "historic" destinies. It could be said that where "history is on the march," thanks to kings, heroes, or empires, the sun is supreme.[8]

Behind the imagery of the light and the sun in the religions of the Near East was the attempt to find meaning and hope for human life in the daily victory of the light over the darkness: the dawn was the harbinger of divine rescue and of eventual salvation. Indeed, the power of the light to bring hope is much older and deeper than mere human history. In responding as they did to the power of the light, the religions of the Near East gave liturgical expression to the yearnings and the stirrings of the protoplasm, the nameless need in the very stuff of life to be sustained by light. Thus John Milton opens the third book of *Paradise Lost:*

> Hail, holy light, offspring of Heaven first-born,
> Or of th' Eternal co-eternal beam,

> May I express thee unblamed? Since God is light,
> And never but in unapproached light
> Dwelt from eternity.[9]

When the World Council of Churches selected "Christ the Light of the World" as the theme for its 1961 Assembly in New Delhi, it placed ecumenical Christian discussion within this long and varied religious tradition. At the same time, it selected an image that has played a major role in the history of specifically Christian theology. Unlike many of the other images in theological history, the image of God and Christ as light can become meaningful even in the twentieth century and even in New Delhi. It is the task of each generation of the church to re-examine the images and metaphors bequeathed to it by the Bible and by subsequent Christian tradition, with a view toward finding those which can serve again as bearers of the Word of God, even though the culture that originally produced them lives no longer. For the warning of Paul Tillich deserves to be heeded:

> . . . symbols cannot be replaced at will; they must be interpreted as long as they are alive. . . . The theologian cannot give a judgment concerning the life or death of the symbols he interprets. This judgment occurs in the consciousness of the living church and has deep roots in the collective unconscious. It happens in the liturgical realm, in personal devotion, in preaching and in teaching, in the activities of the church toward the world, and in the quiet contemplation of its members.[10]

In this book I am undertaking, as a historian of the church and of its thought, to describe a part of this process of judgment. For the exposition of the image of God and Christ as light in early Christian thought I shall be drawing upon the thought and language of Athanasius, (*ca.* 296-373).[11] I am using Athanasius, first of all, because of his intrinsic importance in the history of the early church and because of his continuing relevance to the theology of the modern church. But a more particular reason for concentrating upon Athanasius is the prominent, in fact decisive, role of the image of light in his theology. He summarized and systematized the thought and language of the ancient church about the light of the world. The idea of Christ as light was one of the two or three key images in the case developed by Athanasius for orthodoxy and against Arianism. But the many other features of Christian faith and life to which the writings of Athanasius apply the image of light make it evident that its significance in his thought exceeded the purely Christological. An entire range of theological issues in early Christian thought can take on new meaning when we relate these issues to the image of divine light.

As the notice appearing on page 6 indicates, most of this material was originally delivered as the Gray Lectures at Duke University in October, 1960. In various stages of its revision since that time it has been delivered to the faculty and student body of the Southern Baptist Theological Seminary in Louisville as part of the Gheens Lectures; to clergy of the United Church of Canada at United College, Winnipeg; as the L. W. Anderson Lectures at the Presbyterian College, McGill University, Montreal; to the faculty and student body of the Mennonite Biblical Seminary,

Elkhart, Indiana; to conferences of Lutheran pastors at Omaha, Nebraska, and Ontario, California; as the Swander Lectures at the Lancaster Theological Seminary; as a series of lectures at the University of Notre Dame; and to a retreat of American military chaplains at Berchtesgaden, Germany. The ecumenical and geographical spread of these audiences suggests a conclusion of which I am profoundly persuaded: that in the study of the church fathers, ecumenical Christian theology has huge reserves upon which it should now begin to draw; and that such study, even today, can serve as a means for this generation of Christian believers to repossess the power of their tradition.

This book is dedicated to a dear friend and former colleague, the president of a university that has as its motto Athanasius' favorite passage about the light of the world: "In thy light do we see light."

THE LIGHT OF THE WORLD

1 *GOD AS LIGHT*

"IN THY LIGHT DO WE SEE LIGHT"
is a symbolic statement about God. But when theology
comes to deal with such a symbolic statement of faith from
the Bible, it must be sensitive to the problems inherent in
symbols, images, and figures of speech. From its early be-
ginnings Christian theology has been obliged by both reflection and controversy to become sensitive to these problems, especially as the crude literalism of simple believers
and the ridicule of the cultured despisers of the faith together compelled it to clarify biblical imagery.

The greatest theologian of the ante-Nicene church,
Origen, was compelled to review one biblical image after

another upon which his pagan opponent Celsus had fastened. When the Book of Genesis said that "God rested"; when Isaiah spoke about "the mouth of the Lord"; when the Old Testament asserted that man was created "in the image of God" and the New Testament that Christ was himself "the image of God"—these were all images about God, which were legitimate so long as they were taken as they were meant to be taken. Taken literally, they were nonsense; for God did not need to rest, did not make the air vibrate with his voice, did not have a face of which another could be the image.[1] A little later, answering the charge that according to Christianity God was corporeal by nature, Origen summarized the response of Christian theology to the attempt of Celsus to foist a literal interpretation of biblical imagery upon the church:

> As he endeavors to overthrow notions which we do not maintain, it is superfluous to quote these remarks or to give them any refutation. . . . If he invents out of his own head ideas which he heard from nobody, or, to grant that he heard them from somebody, notions which he derived from some simple and naïve folk who do not know the meaning of the Bible, there is no need to concern ourselves with unnecessary arguments.[2]

When early Christian thought strove to make sense of a biblical image like "Son of God," which was familiar, indeed all too familiar, from pagan myth, it had to rescue this image from the crass connotation that both pagans and heretics were finding in it.[3] Because questions like the nature of propositions, the tests of verification, and "the meaning of meaning" have moved into the center of philo-

sophical inquiry during recent decades, modern readers
may be tempted to forget that these questions, albeit in
the setting of biblical exegesis rather than of semantic
analysis, have engaged some of the best minds of Christen-
dom all along. Indeed, there is probably no concern more
prominent than this in the prolegomena of Christian theologians through the centuries. Faced as he was by the
apologetic assignment of defending the language of the
Bible against pagan attacks just when the church was as-
suming its dominant position in the culture of the Roman
Empire, Athanasius necessarily shared this concern. It was
deepened as he was drawn into the conflict with Arius over
the meaning of images like "Son of God," "Word of God,"
and "radiance of the Father."

In its simplest form, Athanasius' interpretation of the
meaning of images took the form of statements like this:

> In order to express our thought in language, it is necessary
> to make use of an unsatisfactory image taken from
> tangible and familiar objects; for it is rash to pry into
> the incomprehensible nature [of God].[4]

Athanasius was speaking here about the image "light," as
this was applied to the relation between Christ and God.
His explanation was called forth by the Arian attempt to
interpret the words "All things have been delivered to me
by my Father" (Luke 10:22) as proof that the Son was
subordinate to the Father. Although he commented upon
the "admirable precision" of biblical words, he meant not
their literal accuracy as propositions but their clarity as
images. Elsewhere he noted that images like "word,"

"light," and "wisdom" were accommodations to man's inability to grasp the idea of God. It was the function of such images to make it possible for the human mind to form some idea of God, "to the extent that this is attainable."[5] Continuing in the same vein a little later in the same treatise, he addressed himself to the problem of doubt. Faced by the vastness and the mystery of God, man could easily give up the effort to make sense of divine revelation. Yet Athanasius insisted: "In doubt it is better to be silent and to go on believing than to stop believing because of the doubt."[6] He therefore counseled those in doubt to contemplate the images in which the Scriptures described divine being. And since the image under consideration in his discussion was that of Christ as the Logos of God, he turned his exposition to an analysis of both the possibilities and the limits of this image as a way of speaking about the inner life of God. His procedure seems to have been one of excluding from the image those features that did not properly symbolize and of retaining only those which stood for genuine analogies between the Logos of God and the logos of man.

Eventually, perhaps, any created reality could be pressed into service as an image for the divine reality. Indeed,

> . . . everything in time and space has become at some time in the history of religion a symbol for the Holy. And this is naturally so, because everything that is in the world we encounter rests on the ultimate ground of being.[7]

He who made the lamb did make the tiger as well, as William Blake knew; and each of them figures forth some-

thing special about its Creator. Nevertheless, the images
that have evoked the deepest thought and the bitterest
conflict in Christian history have been either derived
directly from the language of the Bible or at least developed
by the Christian tradition in its interpretation of that language. To Athanasius, it has been pointed out, tradition
"is not an indefinite source of knowledge, independent of
Scripture. Not only does he insist upon the sufficiency of
Scripture . . . , he does not strictly distinguish tradition
and Scripture."[8] Scripture and tradition provided him with
images, which, he said, were like the cherubim, spreading
their wings to cover what lay beyond. The content of this
tradition of faith was, therefore, to be measured not by
the wisdom of man, but by the hearing of faith.[9]

Because it was impossible for any creature to exhaust
the inexpressible nature of God, the images handed down
by Scripture and tradition were the place for the theologian
to begin his reflection. Ordinarily these images were drawn
from the natural realm and were used to represent the moral
choices of men. Thus the Old Testament urged men not
to be like horses and mules, and the New Testament told
them that they should be like doves and serpents.[10] But
moral admonition was not the only purpose for which the
Bible employed images. They were especially important as
ways of speaking about the divine reality. Images like
"fountain" or "radiance" were a device for protecting man
from the danger of speaking presumptuously about God.
It was their intention to make it "lawful . . . to speak more
plainly, and to speak without danger, and to think legiti-
mately" about matters that could not be comprehended in

speech.[11] Athanasius appears to have meant that biblical imagery revealed and concealed at the same time, thus protecting human speculation from the danger of going too far. By their very nature such images precluded a "physical interpretation [*logismos sōmatikos*]" and compelled the biblical expositor to transcend the literal sense of the words "radiance" and "light."[12] This was the only way such images would permit themselves to be interpreted. Not, then, to paralyze reflective thinking, but to protect and simultaneously to stimulate it was the function of the images in biblical language.

The most precise and technical term that Athanasius employed for these images was the Greek word *paradeigma*, which may be translated as "pattern." The term had been used by Plato for his ideal city, "laid up as a pattern in heaven, which he who desires may behold, and beholding, may set his own house in order."[13] All the Platonic ideas were "as it were, patterns fixed in nature, and other things are like them and resemblances of them."[14] Perhaps the closest that Athanasius came to this notion of *paradeigma* was in his youthful apologetic, where he wrote:

> The good has being, while the evil does not have being. By "the things that have being," therefore, I mean the things that are good, inasmuch as they have their patterns [*paradeigmata*] in the God-who-is.[15]

But it seems that in his more mature works Athanasius came to reserve the term *paradeigma* for those images, like that of "light" and "radiance," in which the Bible spoke to reveal the way and will of God to man.[16] Here as elsewhere in the history of Christian thought, a term like *paradeigma*, originally borrowed from metaphysics, came eventually to acquire connotations that were more specifically exegetical. It must be added, of course, that the process has sometimes moved in the opposite direction as well.[17]

As he worked with the *paradeigmata*, the theologian was not to forget their basic inadequacy. They continued to be dim in comparison with the ultimate for which they stood. Yet the point of their use was that they were not so dim as to justify pagans and heretics in their literal exegesis of biblical imagery. Biblical images were always at least clear enough to make their symbolic, nonliteral character evident. Here Athanasius could take good advantage of the work of his predecessors, especially that of Origen. At the beginning of this chapter we referred to Origen's defense of the nonliteral meaning of biblical imagery against the distortions of Celsus. One biblical image that evoked the ridicule of pagan thinkers was "Son of God" or "offspring of God." But by the time Athanasius took up the battle against Arianism, this ridicule had received its due refutation from Origen and other apologists. Arius and his followers had no choice, therefore, but to admit that "offspring of God" could be applied to Christ only in a nonliteral sense. And Athanasius was able to capitalize upon this situation and to argue that other Christological images like "radiance," as well as later terms like *homoousios,* had to be interpreted by the same hermeneutical rules that applied to "offspring." "Why should we," he argued, "understand 'offspring' and 'son' in a non-physical way, but interpret *homoousios* in a physical way?"[18]

A literal interpretation of a biblical image like "offspring" or "begotten" claimed to be correct on the grounds that it found more than the "merely symbolic" meaning in such an image, but actually it found far less. To equate the begetting of the Son of God with human procreation was not to transcend the image, but to debase the image and to blaspheme God. For the creation of man out of nothing there were at least some natural parallels, and the Bible used these to convey the meaning of creation. But for the "begetting" of the Son of God by the Father there could be no parallels, only *paradeigmata;* for "no one knows the Son except the Father, and no one knows the Father except the Son and any one to whom the Son chooses to reveal him" (Matt. 11:27). Therefore biblical *paradeigmata* like "radiance" or "fountain" were the basis for an explication of what the Bible meant when it said that God had "begotten" a son.

> The saints, wanting us to understand them this way, have given us such *paradeigmata*. Is it not out of place and irreligious, when the Scriptures contain such images [*eikonas*], to base our thinking about the Lord upon others that are neither written down [in Scripture] nor conducive to piety?[19]

On this basis the meaning of "begetting," and for that matter of *homoousios* as well, could be decided by a theological method that was faithful to the intention of the sacred writers.

This theological method, which Athanasius advocated in his discussion of the problem of biblical *paradeigmata* and which he himself practiced in his constructive and polemical writings, I shall call in one phrase "the collation of biblical images." Professor Paul Minear's description of his own procedure has much in common with this Athanasian method. Minear distinguishes three types of thinking that are required in the interpretation and collation of biblical images:

> The first is synoptic thinking, by which I mean a thinking that embraces all of the images at once, seeing them together in a single panorama and reacting to them all. The second type is reciprocal thinking, by which I mean the effort to think one image into another, to make them almost yet not quite interchangeable, to see how the same meanings flow back and forth from one idiom to the other. The third type might be called retroactive or depth thinking. By this I mean the effort to recover what was in the mind of the author before he said "church" or "saints" or "body of Christ."[20]

All three of these types of thinking were at work in the theology of Athanasius. He took his start from what Minear calls "major" images in Scripture and tradition. These he laid alongside one another, to see what each of them could contribute to the total theological understanding. Thus he sorted out what was *sign*ificant in these signs from those features that did not convey meaning. As we shall see below,[21] this method of collation enabled Athanasius to set "the light of the world" into the context of other biblical images for Jesus Christ and thus to discover what each of these images added and where it needed the support and clarification of other ways of speaking. From this Athanasius could proceed to the formulation of theological terms and entire propositions.

Such terms and propositions, however, could be genuinely biblical even if they did not come directly from the Bible. It was Athanasius, after all, who defended the legitimacy of the creed of Nicaea and of its term *homoousios* even though he himself had been reluctant to use it in his earlier work.[22] Therefore he could not simple-mindedly equate biblical theology with biblical language. He knew that a heretic could express his heresy in purely biblical terminology; on the other hand, it was possible for one to be orthodox in theology even though one's terminology were not biblical in origin.[23] In addition, Athanasius recognized that "someone from among the orthodox believers might, in his naïveté [*haplousteron*]," use heretical terminology, but that his orthodox intention would overcome his rather unfortunate expression.[24] Therefore Athanasius counseled the warring factions in the church of Antioch to reunite, and he warned them against a logomachy that would destroy the unity of the church on account of phraseology.[25] Of those who accepted the content of the creed of Nicaea but who boggled at the term *homoousios* because of its heretical origin or its strangeness, Athanasius found himself able to say:

> We do not attack them here as Ariomaniacs, nor as opponents of the fathers; but we discuss the issue with them as brethren with brethren, who mean what we mean and are disputing only about terminology.[26]

Now among the images for Christ that had been handed down by Scripture and tradition for the theologian's reflection, the image of the light and the radiance was as-

surely one of the more important. As Athanasius himself
put it, "all [the saints] proclaim him as the radiance."[27]
And G. L. Prestige has called the image of light and
radiance "the traditional way of expressing the divine
unity."[28] One of the earliest known Christian hymns was
the *Phōs hilaron*, which hailed Christ as

> Serene light of the Holy Glory
> Of the Father Everlasting
> Jesus Christ.[29]

Because of its prominence in Scripture and in the liturgical
tradition, the image of light and radiance might be expected to appear often in the writings of Athanasius. But
because of his sensitivity to the problem of biblical
imagery, we may safely judge at the same time that he
would not merely play with the image rhetorically or hold
forth dithyrambically on the glories of the uncreated light.
On the contrary, he made a precise effort—more precise
perhaps than the effort of most of his predecessors or con-
temporaries—to locate the image "light" within the
imagery of the Scriptures about Christ and thus to add its
value as a *paradeigma* to all that the Scriptures, through
other *paradeigmata*, had to say about the relation between
Christ and the Father. In short, light was no "mere image"
to Athanasius, because for Athanasius there was nothing
mere about an image.

"God is light," then, is a symbolic statement about God.
Were all statements about God symbolic according to Athanasius, or was it possible to speak of God nonsymboli-
cally?[30] The answer of Athanasius to this question was

called forth by the analogies that his Arian opponents were drawing between divine and human sonship. They admitted, he said, that God as Creator could not be comprehended from the analogy of human creativity. Why, then, should God as Father be comprehended from the analogy of human fatherhood?

> If the very notion of God transcends such thoughts; and if, as soon as he hears [the name "God"], a man recognizes that [God] has being, not as we have being, but as God; and that God creates, yet not as men create, but as God—then it is plain also that He begets not as men beget, but begets as God. For God is not the imitator of man. On the contrary, because God also is properly and truly the Father of his Son, we men are also called the fathers of our own children. For from him "every fatherhood in heaven and on earth is named" [Eph. 3:15].[31]

This interpretation of the words from Ephesians, which has found new support in our own time,[32] meant that when God was called "Father," this was not, strictly speaking, a symbolic statement at all. For to God alone could the term "father" be applied in the most precise and nonsymbolic use of the word. Although men too could be fathers, they had been sons first; before becoming originators, they themselves had been originated. Because "father" meant "giver of life," it was not accurate to say that divine fatherhood was figurative and symbolic while human fatherhood was the archetype; for that amounted to a reversal of the positions of Creator and creature.[33]

The relative positions of Creator and creature led Athanasius to draw this implication:

God creates, and it is said of men that they create too.
Thus God is he-who-is [*ōn*]. Men are also said to be,
because they have received this possession from God. . . .
Men cannot be of themselves . . . , but God is he who is
of himself.[34]

And from this it followed necessarily that "we need only
hear about God to know and perceive that he is he-who-is
[*ho ōn*]."[35] The use of the verb "to be" regarding any
creature ascribed to it a being that was dependent and
derivative. To God, and to God alone, was it proper to
ascribe "being" in the precise sense. The roots of this Athanasian doctrine lay in the Platonic notion that human life
was an imitation (*mimēsis*) of the divine life.[36] According
to Athanasius, the relation between Christ and the Father
was to be the exemplar (*typos*), while men acquired their
sonship and their virtue "by imitation [*kata mimēsin*]."[37]
Thus the cosmological doctrine of imitation in Platonism
was combined with biblical accents.[38] From the use of
images and metaphors in the writings of Athanasius it
seems fair to conclude that this fundamental insight quali-
fied all his statements about God. Thus God was the Father
of all fathers, giving meaning to the fatherhood of men
because he himself was *ho ōn*, in whose true being the
creatures participated for their own being.

The image of God as light conformed to this general
axiom about images for the divine reality. At one level of
discourse it was accurate to say that the statement "God
is light" was symbolic. Yet this did not mean that one
already knew, from some source or other apart from God,
what light was, and that one then attributed some quality

of this light to God. On the contrary, God was uncreated light, the light that illumined every other light, himself the ultimate source of every illumination in his universe. Because, as Athanasius quoted the New Testament, "our God is light"[39] and because, as he never tired of repeating, the Son of God was the "radiance of the Father," he felt warranted in drawing the conclusion:

> ... we may see in the Son the Spirit also by whom we are enlightened. "That he may give you," it says [Eph. 1:17], "the Spirit of wisdom and of revelation in the knowledge of him, having the eyes of your hearts enlightened." But when we are enlightened by the Spirit, it is Christ who in him enlightens us. For it says [John 1:9]: "There was the true light which enlightens every man coming into the world."[40]

As the true and uncreated light in whom there was neither shadow nor turning, God was independent of all his creatures. This doctrine of God as the absolute, who did not need his creatures and was not affected by them, stood in the thought of Athanasius as an axiom. What Werner Elert says of Tertullian applied even more to Athanasius:

> The principle of the impassibility, the *apatheia*, of God, arises here as a sheer axiom, for which no attempt is even made to supply biblical proof. It was no longer new in Christian theology as this was developing. . . . Originally this theology was in the process of basing its picture of God upon the picture of Christ, but that has now passed. . . . From now on the Platonic *apatheia* of God constitutes the a priori presupposition of the entire conception of God in ecclesiastical orthodoxy.[41]

The proof for this principle in Athanasius came not alone from Scripture and from the Christian tradition, but even more from common sense and from the universally accepted views of the time. Greek poets and Cynical philosophers were authorities for the axiom that God was the absolute.[42] It was, Athanasius said, "an admitted truth about God [*peri theou logos*] that he stands in need of nothing, but is self-sufficient and filled with himself."[43] He could base an argument against the Arians upon "the very notion of God," whose implications a man would recognize immediately upon hearing the name "God."[44] He called it "a principle of natural philosophy [*logos physikos*] that that which is single and complete is superior to those things which are diverse."[45]

Acknowledged though it was even by pagan thought and self-evident though it was to anyone who did not refuse to see it, this axiom was substantiated by the Scriptures as well. Athanasius blended natural theology and revealed theology in his arguments for this axiom. No one could deny, he maintained, that those things which once took a beginning were therefore mutable; this was, presumably, a "principle of natural philosophy." But then he immediately went on to verify this principle from three biblical teachings: that the evil angels fell; that Adam disobeyed; and that all things needed the grace of the Logos. "But that which is mutable," he concluded from all this evidence, "cannot be like God, who is truly immutable, any more than that which is created can be like its creator."[46] In this subtle way the Greek notion of God as the absolute came to be identified with the biblical idea of the sovereignty of God. As later discussion will show, this identification compelled theologians like Athanasius to deal with the question: If Christ is truly God, how can the *apatheia* of God be reconciled with the sufferings of Christ on the cross? This doctrine of the absolute led, as Whitehead put it, "to the concept of an entirely static God, with eminent reality, in relation to an entirely fluent world, with deficient reality . . . the notions of a static God condescending to the world, and of a world *either* thoroughly fluent, *or* accidentally static, but finally fluent."[47]

In this entire development, as we have seen, the image of God as light played a fateful role. For the sun was eternal to many of the ancients, the inexhaustibility of its light a continuing miracle. When God was said to be light, this made him a shimmering reality beyond the world, unaffected by the world, a reality that could affect the world only by sending a radiance down upon the world. Adapted to the uses of Christian devotion and theology, this image became fundamental in the language of the church fathers about the relation of God to the world (as Chapter 2 will show) and about the relation of God to Christ (as Chapter 3 will show).

2 *GOD'S DARKLING WORLD*

"IN THY LIGHT DO WE SEE LIGHT"
is not only a symbolic way of speaking about God. It is
also a confession of the faith that this world is God's world,
illumined by his creation and revelation. Thus in the
imagery of the Bible "light" is both a term for God and the
name of the first among the creatures of God. *Fiat lux*
provided Christian theology from the very outset with an
image for speaking at the same time about the nature of
God himself and about the meaning of his creative act.
The language of the Bible spoke about God as light and the
world as light, not merely about God as light and the
world as darkness. Consideration of this usage seemed al-

most to compel Christian theologians to look for analogies between Creator and creature, and not merely to emphasize the discontinuity between the holy Creator and the fallen creature.[1]

As Athanasius took up the doctrine of creation, therefore, the image of light often supplied him with the proper language. He declared, for example, that a denial of the doctrine of creation and of the cross of Christ as "the healing of creation" was as foolish as a denial of the existence of the sun simply because it was momentarily obscured by clouds.[2] For if the light was good and if the sun, from which the light proceeded, was nobler yet, then the presence of hope and of the knowledge of God in the world pointed beyond itself to its source in God and in his eternal Logos, who was the orderer of it all. The relation between the light and the radiance, which determined much of the Christology of the mature Athanasius, thus helped to shape his doctrine of creation as well. It enabled him, even in his early writings, to argue from everyday experience to Christian doctrine, providing him with a basic analogy by which his entire world view was shaped.

The primordial experience of the warmth and power of the light similarly enabled Athanasius to contrast the limited creative power of the universe and its parts with the unlimited creative power of God, which was within the universe yet beyond it. This contrast between the creativity of the Creator and the derivative creativity of the creature became important in the controversy over the person of Christ. Although the Arians were unwilling to identify Christ with the Creator in his essence, as the *homoousios*

at Nicaea did, they were willing to acknowledge that Christ
was deserving of worship. On this ground Athanasius accused them of reviving the Gnostic worship of the angels
and of lumping Christ with the angels as the highest among
creatures, "as Valentinus, Marcion, and Basilides believed,
whose partisans you are."[3] But since the angels were themselves creatures, made out of nothing, they could not create
in the proper sense of the word. The Logos, therefore,
could not be in the same class as the angels. For if the Logos
belonged to the category "creature" rather than to the
category "Creator," even if he were the highest among the
creatures, it would have been impossible for all things to
be created out of nothing by the Logos; for he himself
would be created out of nothing. Again, it was the image
of the light that supported the argument:

> Being a creature, the sun will never make nonbeing into
> being. Man will not shape man, nor a stone form stone,
> nor wood give growth to wood. It is God who shapes
> man in the womb, who establishes the mountains, and who
> makes wood to grow. But man, being capable of knowl-
> edge, assembles and arranges this material and works
> existing things, as he has been taught.[4]

It was consistent with this Athanasian teaching when the
so-called *Fourth Discourse against the Arians*, which was
ascribed to Athanasius although it was probably written
by someone else, reasoned that because Christ was the light
of the world, he must also have been the one by whom
the world was originally made.[5] The image of light was
so basic to the thought of Athanasius because in reflection
upon it he could formulate his entire doctrine of creation.

The image of light was also eminently suitable to the needs of Athanasius as he proceeded to discuss the doctrine of the fall.[6] This world was indeed God's world, but it was God's darkling world. The fall had not extinguished the light of God, nor had it plunged the entire world into darkness; as we shall see, this conviction never forsook Athanasius. Objectively speaking, the world which participated in reality, participated in God. But subjectively speaking, as far as man the sinner was concerned, the world was as dark as if there were no light any more. Of all the images that Athanasius found in Scripture and tradition for this plight of man, none was more effective than his picture of the man who was unable to see the light even though it was still there:

> If someone were to plunge into the depths, he would no longer see the light nor the things that are visible by the light; for his eyes would be turned downward, and the water would be all above him. Perceiving only what is in the depths, he would suppose that nothing else exists, but that what is evident to him is the only true reality.[7]

Such was the condition of man since the fall into sin. His world had become a darkling world because he refused to face the light of God. Like a bat, he pretended that this darkling world was the only world there was, and that the light was no more than an illusion.

The sinner's interpretation of light and darkness in the world was, of course, a reversal of reality. In fact, the light was real and the darkness was an illusion. Athanasius likened man's condition to that of a man who would close his eyes tightly when the sun was shining. Such a man would "suppose that there is darkness where no darkness exists."[8] If such a man acted on his experience and walked about with his eyes closed against the sunlight, he would stumble and fall just as though the darkness were real. The simile continues:

> So also the human soul, tightly closing its eyes, by which it can see God, has imagined evil for itself. Moving [about] in this, it does not recognize that when it supposes that it is doing something, it is doing nothing.

For God was light, and God was being; darkness was the realm of nonbeing. But when the human soul treated non-being as though it were being and reversed the positions of darkness and light, it gave to darkness a power over man that did not belong to darkness by right. Darkness was able to usurp this power because of the false faith of those who had deliberately shut their eyes against the light of being.

The threat of sin was the danger that man would be dragged, or would voluntarily slide, back into nonbeing. He had originally been created out of nothing, out of that which had no being. This origin constituted a continuing danger to man; for "man is by nature mortal, since he is made out of what is not."[9] But this natural propensity to death and dissolution was checked by his participation in the image of God. For God was he-who-is (*ho ōn*),[10] and man could have kept his immortality if he had kept intact his knowledge of a being who was beyond corruption and transiency, thus beyond death. It appears to have been the teaching of Athanasius, despite certain statements that seem inconsistent with this, that the darkness had no authority over those who were the children of the light unless they permitted it to have that authority by pretending that darkness had reality and thus obeying darkness rather than light. Apparently he meant that the only reality that darkness could claim was subjective; for God was light, and by participating in his reality the world participated in his light.

One of the most persistent themes of Athanasian apologetics was this defense of the intrinsic goodness of reality against its detractors. And a frequent image for this defense was the metaphor of the light. If one accepted the proposition that the Logos of God was present throughout the universe, one would likewise have to grant that the entire universe was both illumined and moved by the Logos, from whom there came the light and movement and life of all things. [11] Again, it was the Logos that granted light and life to the universe; and because the Logos had illumined all things, visible and invisible, it was the holy Logos of the Father that held them all together.[12] This goodness of all reality was built into the very structure of being by the Logos, who was the principle of life, light, and movement. Committed as he was to the defense of the salvation wrought by Christ, Athanasius did not, like Tertullian and some later theologians, find it necessary to denigrate nature in order to glorify grace. On the contrary, he took his stand as the defender of the goodness of nature against its detractors; for this defense of the goodness in all of reality was at the same time an act of praise for the God of grace. There was

not only revelation in the creation; there was even grace in
the creation:

> He who is good cannot grudge anything. Therefore he
> does not grudge even being, but he wants everything to
> be, so that he can show his steadfast love. He saw that all
> created nature, if left to its own principles, was in flux
> and subject to dissolution. To prevent this and to keep
> the universe from disintegrating back into nonbeing, he
> made all things by his very own eternal Logos and en-
> dowed the creation with being.[13]. . . He guides it by the
> Logos, so that by the direction, providence, and ordering
> of the Logos, the creation may be illumined and enabled
> to abide always securely.[14]

Therefore Augustine's formula would suit Athanasius'
teaching as well: being, as being, was good, because it was
a participation in the being of God; and it was purposeful
because it had a share in the Logos of God. The darkness
of sin had fallen over the world; and the minds of men,
once illumined by the knowledge of God, had been obscured
by ignorance and doubt. But the world was still God's
world. Evidence for this came from the creation outside
of man. The sun, moon, and stars had not forsaken their
established order. They continued to shine as the lights of
God, for "nothing in creation except man" had perverted
its idea of God.[15] At one point Athanasius even went a
whole step further to declare that the sun was illumined by
the Logos and thus was enabled to spread its radiance over
the world, and that it was also from the Logos that the
moon had received its allotted period for shining.[16] Because
the Logos was the principle of creative order in the universe,

created beings fulfilled themselves by finding the power of their being in him. No created being would have had an established existence if it had not been for the Logos. Thus for Athanasius the image of light was fundamental to creation. It was as though the psalm were paraphrased: "In thy [uncreated] light do we see [created] light."

If Athanasius was so persuaded of the essential goodness of God's darkling world despite the sin of man, he could not avoid the problem of the relation between the light of Christ and the other lights of religion that had illumined the minds of men. His solution of this problem appears to have been a twofold one: a refusal to concede that the lights of religion were lights at all, and at the same time a readiness to make huge concessions to the theoretical power of the unaided human eye to see the light of God. This twofold solution enabled him to denounce the gods of the nations as "gods falsely so-called [*pseudōnymoi theoi*]"[17] even while he was defending the essential goodness of the created world after man's fall into sin. The polemic against the darkness of the "gods falsely so-called" occupied not only the apologetic work of the youthful Athanasius, but his maturer work as well. Speaking through the mouth of the hermit Antony, Athanasius denounced paganism for refusing to content itself with admiration for the created world and "rendering service to the creature in place of the God who created all."[18] The demonic apparitions that underlay pagan worship gave the appearance of genuine light and thus could easily deceive those who were searching for light. In reality they were the manifestation of what Milton called "darkness visible."

Therefore Antony admonished his hearers:

> It is not true light which appears in them [the appari-
> tions]. Rather they are a mere beginning and semblance
> of the fire prepared for them; and it is with that in which
> they will be burned that they try to terrify mankind.[19]

Despite its devotion, the worship of these demonic deities
was atheism, for it was a denial of the only true God, "the
Father of our Lord Jesus Christ."[20]

Behind this conventional equation of paganism with
atheism[21] stood a more profound analysis of the meaning
of polytheism, an analysis that played a significant part in
the controversy with Arianism as well. Paganism worshiped
the light under the form of the lights, ascribing divinity
to the sun, the moon, and the stars. But the very multi-
plicity of these lights disqualified them as pretenders to
the title "the light of the world." How was it possible for
authentic deity to take part in the competition and mutual
opposition that characterized the heavenly lights?

> When the sun is under the earth, the earth's shadow
> makes his light invisible, while by day the sun hides the
> moon by the brilliancy of his light. . . . If they were gods,
> they ought not to be defeated and obscured by one an-
> other, but always to co-exist, and to discharge their respec-
> tive functions simultaneously. Both by night and by day
> the sun and the moon and the rest of the band of stars
> ought to shine equally together, and give their light to
> all, so that all things might be illumined by them.[22]

If there was a divine principle of sovereignty, it had to
be a single principle; for creatures, with their circumscribed
sovereignty, could be many, but the Creator, with ultimate

sovereignty, could be only one. Or, as Athanasius put it in an axiom, "polytheism is atheism . . . , polyarchy is necessarily anarchy."[23] When the Arians contended that a secondary principle, the Logos, was less than the Creator but more than the creatures, they could logically be accused of reintroducing polytheism.[24]

The Arians claimed, however, to be combating the polytheism they found to be implicit in the Athanasian doctrine of the Trinity. In support of their position they cited the declarations of the Lord in the Old Testament against the gods of the nations. They argued that declarations like "the Lord is God; there is no other besides him" (Deut. 4:35) implied that the Son of God was not God in the same sense as the Father. Thus they distinguished God as the light from all other lights, also from the Son of God as light. To this distinction, as our next chapter will show, Athanasius replied with a careful delineation of the close connection between light and radiance. He also distinguished carefully between the radiance of the true light and all other lights:

> If, during the day, with the sun shining, a man were to paint a crude picture on a piece of wood, which did not even look like light; if he were to call that picture the source of the light; and if the sun were to look at this [picture] and say, "Only I am the light of the day, and there is no other light of the day but I"—the sun would be saying this not about its own radiance, but about the error arising from the wooden image.[25]

God the light and Christ his radiance had nothing in common with the lights falsely so-called.

Yet this denunciation of paganism as darkness rather than light was only half of Athanasius' answer to the problem of the light and the lights, for at the same time he argued that the light of creation could illumine the mind to see God. Even in a treatise in defense of Nicene orthodoxy against Arianism, Athanasius could declare that "creation is sufficient [to confirm] the knowledge that there is a God and that there is a providence." Then he went on to say:

> We learn from [the creatures] without asking for voices, but hearing the Scriptures we believe. As we look at the order and the harmony of all things, we recognize that he is maker and ruler and God of all things; and we grasp his wondrous providence and sovereignty over all things.[26]

The reference to "hearing the Scriptures" in the midst of this discussion of natural theology is puzzling. Evidently he did not mean to say that the contemplation of the order in the universe was possible only on the basis of the revelation in the Scriptures, for the very point of his argument was the evidence of creation for the providence of God. From the context he seems to have meant merely that this evidence and the testimony of the Scriptures were in agreement. This was an elaboration of his idea that the knowledge of the Creator gained from the scrutiny of the heavens and the knowledge communicated to man through the law and the prophets were identical and that therefore the prophets were the teachers of all nations, not only of the Jews.[27]

From the creation it was possible to infer not only the existence of God but the oneness of God as well. Contemplation of the universe and of its order led to the

conclusion that behind its many lights and various move-
ments was one ruler and king, "moving and illumining all
by his own light."[28] The gods of classical polytheism and
the astral deities of Hellenistic religion had no light, and
indeed no being; for the light of the stars was from the one
God of heaven and earth, who was himself the true light
and the source of all light. It was by his light that men were
enabled to see light. The logic of this argument could be
carried even further. Athanasius could even contend that
not alone the being of God, not alone the oneness of God,
but even the Logos of God could be perceived on the basis
of a contemplation of the heavens and their light. "Looking
up into heaven and seeing its order [*kosmos*] and the light
of the stars, one can infer the Logos, who orders these
[*ton tauta diakosmounta Logon*]."[29] Rational structure pre-
supposed a rational principle; an ordered cosmos indicated
the presence and power of an ordering Logos; the light of
the stars bore witness to the light of the universe. Such a
"natural theology" therefore served to reinforce the
theology of the Logos, who was both the light of creation and the light of redemption, neither without the other.

Nor may such bold statements be dismissed as expres-
sions of rhetorical exuberance, to be sloughed off as Athanasius became more cautious through his battles against
heresy. In the very midst of a vigorous attack upon Arianism, he still remembered the revelation in the creation.
Although he was attacking Arianism as a relapse into the
polytheistic natural religion of paganism and a betrayal
of the Christian doctrine of redemption, this did not push
Athanasius into the opposite extreme of obliterating crea-

tion for the sake of exalting redemption. On the contrary, he deliberately sought to put himself into the position of defending both redemption by the Logos and creation by the Logos against the Arian contention that the Logos was merely the first among the creatures of God.

> The works of the true Logos are evident to all, so that by analogy [*analogōs*] he can be contemplated on the basis of them. For just as when we see the creation, we think of God as the one who created it, so when we see that in the creatures there is nothing disordered, but that everything moves and abides with order and providence, we infer that it is the Logos of God who is over all and governs all.[30]

The Logos, whom faith had come to know in Jesus Christ as the light of the world, had been the light of the world all along.

This interpretation of the world as God's darkling world formed the necessary foundation for everything that Athanasius had to say about Christ as the light of the world. Because the world was God's world, created by his Logos and still illumined by his light, it was *possible* for the Logos to become man. But because God's world was God's darkling world, where men had blinded themselves to his true light, it was also *necessary* for the Logos to become man and to enlighten the hearts and minds of men. By his illumination men were enabled to see the world as it truly was and not as the cataracts of their sin had caused them to view it: "In thy light do we see light."

3 THE RADIANCE

OF THE FATHER

"IN THY LIGHT DO WE SEE LIGHT":
Although this verse from the psalms held many implications for Athanasius, the primary meaning that he found in it was its meaning for the doctrine of the person of Christ. It meant to him that in Christ as the light from God men could, by revelation, see God as light, and that Christ as the radiance of the Father was coequal with God as light. This was not the principal passage from the Old Testament in the panoply of Athanasius against the Arians. That distinction appears to have belonged—strange though this seems at first to modern judgment—to the eighth chapter of the Book of Proverbs. In conjunction with the prologue

to the Gospel of John, which was its New Testament counterpart, the eighth chapter of Proverbs was central to the exposition, speculation, and argumentation about the person of Christ during the third, fourth, and fifth centuries.[1] There was, however, a second echelon of biblical testimonies which sometimes illustrated and sometimes corroborated the evidence of the several passages that were truly crucial and decisive.[2] In this second echelon the words of the psalmist, "In thy light do we see light," had their place.

Secondary though the importance of Psalm 36:9 may have been as an individual biblical testimony about the person of Christ, the image of light and radiance, which it contains, was of primary significance for the entire ancient church. Indeed, this image took its place just behind the image of Christ as the Logos of God and the image of Christ as the Son of God, contributing its special elements to the theological thought and language of fathers like Athanasius and helping eventually—a generation after Athanasius—to formulate the orthodox doctrine of the holy and undivided Trinity. Thus the history of the development of the doctrines of the Trinity and of the person of Christ in the first five centuries could conceivably be written around the several explanations and expositions of this image, as the interpretation of the image of light advanced from the naïve and unreflective suggestions of the early fathers to the sophistication of the late Greek fathers, in whose thought "the old sun-and-radiance metaphor is gathered up and preserved in the new formulation of the coinherence."[3] Through the evolution of the image of light and radiance from rhetorical naïveté to theological sublety and precision, the dogma of the Trinity came of age, and for this evolution Athanasius deserves a good share of the credit.

The earliest application of the image of light to the relation between Christ and the Father occurred in the New Testament itself. The Epistle to the Hebrews called Christ the *apaugasma*, the radiance, brightness, or reflection, of the glory of the Father.[4] In the setting of the argument being developed by the opening paragraphs of the epistle and in combination with the other language employed there, the image of Christ as the radiance of the Father suggested two distinct theological motifs, the derivation of Christ from the Father and the identity of Christ with the Father. As the subsequent history of this image demonstrated, the problem was: How could both the derivation and the identity receive full justice in a single theological formula? To that problem much of the history of Christian thought about the image of light and the related image of fire was devoted. Only gradually did the fuller implications of the image become explicit for thinkers of the church like Athanasius, as more profound reflection upon it eliminated the simpler and rather superficial conclusions it had originally suggested.

An examination of how the image of radiance and light was used by some Christian theologians in the second and third centuries indicates that the derivation of Christ from the Father was its early and obvious meaning, but that the concept of identity between the light and the radiance began to impose itself upon the fathers as they probed more deeply into the image. Justin Martyr and his pupil Tatian, for example, took it to mean that as fire could be ignited from fire without diminishing that from which it was taken, so the Son was derived from the Father without a loss in the deity of the Father.[5] Here the accent was not so much upon the coessentiality of the Father and the Son as upon the inviolability of the Father despite the generation of the Son. For the purpose of making that point, it was an apt image. But if it was carried beyond this single point of analogy, it quickly led to conclusions that threatened the concept of coessentiality between the Father and the Son. As Athanasius eventually acknowledged, the image of fire kindled from fire suggested that the new fire or firebrand was something external to the old, created and wrought by it but separate from it.[6] If, for example, something were to be ignited from the heat of the sun, its fire could properly be said to be derived from the sun. Yet if the fire were extinguished, that would not affect the heat of the sun at all. Applied to the relation between God and Christ, the image of fire from fire soon made the Son radically subordinate to the Father, as the creature was subordinate to the Creator.

If the image of light and radiance was to serve the purpose of the church's confession that Christ was "very God of very God," it had to be disengaged from the image of fire from fire. Without intending to support Arian teaching, an orthodox theologian could be beguiled by the image of fire into statements that had a pronouncedly Arian flavor. Thus Dionysius of Alexandria, one of Athanasius' most distinguished predecessors, in the middle of the third century said of the begetting of the Son by the Father: "Life was begotten from life, and it flowed as a river from a well; and from light unquenchable bright light was kindled."[7] Harmless enough in its poetic and rhetorical intent, this declaration, upon more careful examination, began to look like evidence for the Arian doctrine that the Son was less than the Father, and therefore like proof that the tradition of the centuries since the apostles was on the side of Arius rather than of Nicaea. To meet this claim, Athanasius composed an epistle in which he sought to demonstrate that the author of this declaration "opposed the Arian heresy, just as the Council of Nicaea did, and that it is useless for the Arians to slander him by claiming him for their position."[8] Other passages from the writings of Dionysius made clear that he did not intend to use the image of fire from fire to support the Arian doctrine, but that he did use the image of light and radiance to support what was eventually to emerge as the Nicene doctrine.

From one such writing, entitled *Refutation and Defense* (which has unfortunately been lost since), Athanasius quoted an extensive exposition of the image of light and radiance:

> Being the radiance of eternal light, he [the Son] is surely eternal himself; for if the light exists always, it is evident that the radiance, too, exists always. . . . If the sun were eternal, the daylight also would be unending; but since that is not so in fact, the day begins with the sun and ends with the sun. God, however, is eternal light, neither beginning nor ending. Therefore the radiance lies before him and is with him eternally, having no beginning and being eternally begotten.[9]

Other fathers too had to be rescued from the charge that their imprecise use of images like fire and light made them ancestors of Arianism. Not only in his special defense of Dionysius, but in other works as well, Athanasius felt obliged to quote the fathers and by a careful exegesis to show their consensus in support of the orthodox doctrine. A fragment from Origen, for example, asked: "The God who, according to John, is called light (for 'God is light') —when was he ever without a radiance of his very own glory?"[10] Hence, according to Athanasius' exegesis of Origen, the image of light and radiance had to signify that the Son of God was as eternal as God, who could not be without his radiance. And in the same treatise Athanasius quoted Theognostus of Alexandria in support of the contention that the radiance was neither the light itself nor something alien to the light; so the Son of God was distinct from the Father, yet of the same essence with the Father.[11]

From the opposite end of the North African coast along the Mediterranean, from Carthage, came further testimony on the image of the light and the radiance. Tertullian, who was responsible for the origin of much of the theological language of the Western church, made use of this image in his accounts of the person of Christ. In his *Apology*, for example, he asserted: "Christ is spirit from spirit and God from God, as light is kindled from light."[12] This meant, he continued, that God as light suffered no loss through the kindling of the light from him; but it meant also that the Son of God was God and that the two were one. The application of the image of the light to the relation between Christ and the Father was one of the lessons—one of the

few lessons, actually—that Tertullian ascribed to the in-
struction of the Paraclete who spoke to and through the
Montanist movement.[13] It proved that Christ and the Father
were one and that the Son could properly be termed a
"projection [*probolē*]" of the Father, despite the heretical,
Gnostic connotations of that term.[14] Among both Greek-
speaking and Latin-speaking fathers, then, the image of
God as light and Christ as radiance had begun to acquire,
by the end of the third century, the more subtle and profound connotations that Athanasius, following the Council
of Nicaea, recognized in it.

Thus it took its place just one degree below two other
basic images for the relation between Christ and God: the
Son of God and the Logos of God. In the literature on
the history of the doctrine of the person of Christ these
latter two images have claimed the major share of theological and scholarly attention, and with good reason. The
development of the doctrines of the person of Christ and
of the Trinity did consist in the effort of the church to
strip these images of the connotations that did not belong
in a Christian confession and to replace these connotations
with others that were appropriate to Christian theology.
The image "Son of God" carried at least two sets of connotations of which it had to be cleansed if it was to serve as
a reliable bearer of the church's testimony to what God had
done in Jesus as the Christ. Likewise, the image "Logos of
God" connoted two clusters of ideas diametrically opposite
to those connoted by the metaphor "Son of God," but
equally inimical to Christian worship and witness. To understand the significance of the image "radiance of God,"

one must compare and contrast it with these two classic Christian designations for the way Jesus the Christ is related to God. For, like them, it was a device for answering the question of the ancient church, as summarized by Adolf Harnack: "Is the divine that has appeared on earth and reunited man with God identical with the supreme divine, which rules heaven and earth, or is it a demigod?"[15]

From earliest times a favorite Christian term for Jesus as the Christ had been "Son of God." Indeed, the Gospel of Luke made this term a part of the prenatal confession of the angel to the divine mission of Jesus (Luke 1:35): "The child to be born will be called holy, the Son of God." Throughout the New Testament this image was echoed, both in the gospels and in the epistles; and virtually every Christian creed has contained the declaration ascribed to Peter at Caesarea Philippi, that Jesus is "the Christ, the Son of the living God" (Matt. 16:16). The well-nigh universal distribution of this image in early Christian literature guarantees to the phrase "Son of God" a place in any Christian speech about Jesus. It is not surprising, therefore, that its appearances can be documented from the writings of church fathers East and West, Greek and Latin, orthodox and heterodox. Still, as has been indicated, the image "Son of God" was freighted with at least two sets of connotations that prevented it from communicating directly what the Christian faith meant by its confession that Jesus of Nazareth was the Christ of God. And the image of Jesus as the radiance of God, together with other images, served to counterbalance both these sets of connotations; for no one image could carry alone the weight of the Christian revelation and the burden of the Christian confession.

From the reaction of Greek and Roman philosophers to the Christian designation of Jesus as "Son of God" it was clear that Christian thought had great difficulty exorcising this designation of its mythological and superstitious implications. Having spent several centuries on the task of purging their own religion of these implications, the nobler minds of paganism resented the reintroduction of this image into the language of religious thought.[16] This much must be admitted: In spite of the care and precision of Christian theological formulation, the debasement of the metaphor "Son of God" in the piety of Christian people often provided grounds for this resentment. It proved to be even more difficult for Christian theology to purge the image "Son of God" of connotations that suggested the subordination of the Son to the Father. How could one who was derived from another—and that was the irreducible minimum implied by the image of a son—be coequal and coessential with that other? Athananius was aware of this disability in the image, but he would not concede the argument to the Arians on account of the disability. Instead, he invoked other images for the derivation of the Son from the Father, images in which the notion of subordination was not so prominent. Among these the image of light and radiance proved extremely useful. With its aid Athanasius sought to demonstrate that "Son of God" did not reintroduce carnal thoughts into religion and that the radiance of God, though derived, was coequal in light with its source.[17]

Ever since the Christian thought of the second century,

the New Testament image "Logos of God" had been a counterweight to the superstition that so easily beset the image "Son of God," but it, too, created its own special set of problems. If the image "Son of God" almost inevitably lapsed into mythology, the image "Logos of God," with equal inevitability, suggested an abstraction that was hard to identify with the birth, suffering, and death of a Palestinian rabbi. Despite its prominence in the foregoing debates, it did not even appear in the creed adopted at Nicaea. "Logos" suffered from another disadvantage, which was due to the connotations in the notion of a word. A word could not be a self; it only participated in the self-hood and identity of the speaker. At best, his identity could be said to take the form of speech, as it took other forms in action, posture, or gesture. All of these were passing phases of his relation to the world, and of them none was more evanescent than the word. Harnessed to the doctrine of the person of Christ, this image suggested that the one God had taken a variety of forms as he related himself to the world, and that the Logos was merely one of these passing forms or modes of his relation—what came to be known in early Christian thought as the Sabellian heresy.[18]

Although the image "Logos of God" did not appear in the creed adopted at the Council of Nicaea, the image "light from light," which did appear in it, carried out many of the same functions. It too connoted evanescence and seemed too abstract a term for the life of Jesus of Nazareth. At the hands of Athanasius, however, it is acquired a fullness and a precision of meaning that equipped it for use in the doctrine of the person of Christ. Athanasius accused the

Arians of multiplying images, including this one, but of failing to draw out their fuller and deeper implications. Setting himself into contrast with Arianism and into continuity with the tradition of the fathers, Athanasius represented himself as an interpreter of the language of the Scriptures. "Behold," he announced, "we speak confidently on the basis of the divine Scriptures concerning the religious faith and set it up as a light on a candlestick, saying: . . . He is the very stamp of the nature of the Father and light from light and the true image of the essence of the Father."[19]

On this basis Athanasius declared that God the light had never been without his radiance. The Arian doctrine was, he asserted, tantamount to saying that "the divine essence is not fruitful but sterile, a light that does not lighten and a fountain that is dry."[20] Although the Arians were willing to admit that now Christ was the light and radiance of the Father, they claimed that once, before the generation and creation of the Son, God the light had had no radiance or ray. Athanasius' rhetorical reply to this claim was: "He who is God, was he ever not rational [*alogos*]? He who is light, was he ever not radiant?"[21] In keeping with his consistent charge that the Arian doctrine was polytheistic and mythological,[22] Athanasius accused it of interpreting divine fatherhood and sonship mythologically. The Son would be subordinate to the Father, he argued, only if the Father had begotten the Son after the manner attributed to the Olympian deities. The radiance would be less than the light if the light were temporal. But because the light was eternal, it followed that the Son of God was "the image and eternal Logos of the Father, never having not been, but being eternally, as the eternal radiance of a light that is eternal."[23] Athanasius made a similar response to the idea that the Son of God was not of the Father's essence, but had come into being by the will of the Father:

> In the case of the radiance and light one might say that there is no will preceding radiance in the light; but it [the radiance] is its natural offspring, at the pleasure of the light which begat it, not by will and consideration, but in nature and truth. So also in the instance of the Father and the Son, one might rightly say that the Father has love and good pleasure towards the Son and the Son has love and good pleasure towards the Father.[24]

And this love and good pleasure were as eternal as the eternal radiance of the divine light.

Like "Son of God," then, "radiance of God" did convey the derivation of Christ from God. Even as he set forth his arguments rejecting any idea of subordination, Athanasius could say that the Son of God was "his radiance, by whom he enlightens all things and is revealed to whom he wishes."[25] He could also represent the radiance as saying: "The light has given me all places to enlighten, and I do not enlighten of myself, but as the light wills." When he had said this, however, he quickly added the paraphrase: "I am proper to the light, and everything that belongs to the light belongs to me."[26] Despite the paraphrase, the image of Christ as radiance made clear that Christ proceeded from the Father, albeit eternally. For no amount of speculation, whether heretical or orthodox, could be permitted to drain off from images like "Son of God" and

"radiance of God" the very relationship they were intended
to symbolize. This relationship the "Nicene Creed" summarized in the phrases: "God of God, light of light, very
God of very God." Properly understood, the orthodox
doctrine of the Trinity did not eliminate this "of" or "from"
(*ek*), but demanded it, as the image of light and radiance
made clear:

> The God-who-is is eternally. Since the Father always is, his
> radiance also is eternally, because it is his Logos. And
> again, the God-who-is has from himself [*ex autou*] the
> Logos, who also is.[27]

Yet the "from" did not mean "subordinate to": this was
the burden of the case that Athanasius made against the
Arians. "From" meant "of the essence of, of the same
essence as," *homoousios*.[28] For the confirmation of this
meaning the image of Christ as radiance proved very useful
to Athanasius. It helped him to argue that the Son could
not be of a different essence from the Father, as the Arian
doctrine declared. "Will anyone dare to say," he asked,
"that the radiance of the sun is unlike the sun and alien to
it?" On the contrary, anyone who would ponder the
relation between the sun and its radiance would be compelled to admit: "Of course the light and the radiance are
one, and the one is made evident in the other, and the radiance is in the sun, in such a way that anyone who sees the
one sees the other as well."[29] Because Christ as the radiance
was not alien to the essence of the Father but of the same
essence as the Father, the light with which the radiance enlightened every man who came into the world was truly the

light of the Father, not some alien light. Therefore the conclusion followed: "He cannot be out of nothing or be a creature at all, but must be the very offspring of the Father himself, as the radiance from the light."[30]

Only if the radiance was not alien to the essence of God the light, but proper to it, could the essence of God remain undivided and unimpaired.[31] Here again the preoccupation of Athanasius with the philosophical notion of God as the absolute and impassible one asserted itself.[32] So thoroughly had this notion been incorporated into the very definition of the oneness of God that for the thought of Athanasius the biblical insistence upon the unity of God and this concept of the simplicity of God had become virtually synonymous. In keeping with this concept, Athanasius used the image of the light and the radiance to good advantage as he made the point that the eternal begetting of the Son of God did not violate or impair the unity of the divine essence. A man's reason (*logos*), Athanasius argued, belonged to the very essence of the man, because it had always been with him and there had been no time when it was not; so it was with the Logos of God, which was as eternal as God because it belonged to the essence of God. The image of the radiance added its weight to this argument:

> So again we see that the radiance from the sun is proper to it, and the sun's essence is not divided or impaired. Its essence is whole and its radiance perfect and whole, yet without impairing the essence of light, but as a true offspring from it. We understand similarly that the Son is begotten not from without but from the Father; and while the Father remains whole, the expression of his subsistence has his being eternally.[33]

In short, the radiance of God was perfect; but when it was emitted, it left the light of God perfect as well.

Radiance and light had to be inseparable. "If anyone . . . dares to separate the radiance from the light and to say that the radiance is of another essence, let him join Arius in his insanity; for such a person has lost even the semblance of human intelligence."[34] Yet Athanasius had to reckon with the usage of Scripture and tradition, which could speak separately of the Father and of the Son. His insistence upon the inseparability of the two might seem artificial in the face of this usage. To this criticism of his position Athanasius replied that a consideration of the image of light would support his point. For one could speak of the light of the sun without referring explicitly to the sun; and the light of the sun could say of itself: "From the sun I have received the power to illumine all things and to give them growth and strength by the heat that is in me."[35] Still no sane person would be justified in concluding from this that the sun and its light were being separated or that the sun was of a nature different from that of the light. No more justified was it, he reasoned, to separate the nature of Christ from that of the Father, even though one could speak either of Christ or of the Father without referring explicitly to the other. When the Epistle to the Hebrews called Christ the radiance or reflection of the Father, this meant "that the radiance cannot be separated from the light, but is proper to it by nature and coexistent with it."[36]

For this coexistence the most comprehensive term was *homoousios*, "of the same essence," adopted at the Council of Nicaea. The term was difficult to liberate from its setting in the language of Manichaeans, Sabellians, and other heretics.[37] Athanasius tended to avoid the term in his early books; even in his later books he used it more rarely than his association with it in the textbooks might lead one to believe.[38] But when he came to the defense of Nicaea, he did not hesitate to uphold this terminology. Only if someone were willing to maintain that the sun and its radiance were two separate lights or two different essences, would he have a right to object to the term *homoousios;* for the Father and the Son were even less divisible than the sun and its radiance.[39] The sun and its radiance were one light, though the sun and its radiance were two. "So also the godhead of the Son is the Father's; whence also it is indivisible. And thus there is one God, and none other than he."[40] Once more the image of the light and the radiance provided Athanasius with a key argument for the support of Nicene orthodoxy, as he summarized his brief a little later in the same treatise:

> What the light enlightens, that the radiance irradiates; and what the radiance irradiates, from the light is its enlightenment. Thus also when the Son is beheld, so is the Father, for he is the Father's radiance; and hence the Father and the Son are one.[41]

Therefore Christ was "very light, the light itself," as Athanasius phrased it in his earliest book.[42]

In the companion volume to that book Athanasius put the image of the light to yet another use for the theological interpretation of Christ. He was answering the objection of pagan critics that if the divine Logos had truly been incarnate in a human body, this would have defiled his purity and limited his divinity. On the contrary, Athanasius

argued; for the sun in the sky was not defiled when it
touched bodies on earth, nor was it extinguished by darkness, but it cleansed the bodies and illumined the darkness.
So it was with the Logos. Coming into a human body, he
had not been defiled by it; on the contrary, he had cleansed
it and communicated his own immortality to it.[43] At this
point Athanasius had not thought out the fuller implications of this image for the doctrine of salvation, and therefore he did not develop the image here. As Chapter 4 will
show, his mature thought returned to the idea of salvation
as illumination, which made it possible for him to use the
image of the light as a way of speaking both about the
person of Christ and about the work of Christ.

In its role as a way of speaking about the person of Christ,
this image helped Athanasius to make certain points that
would have been more difficult to make without it. It also
had certain inherent weaknesses, which he does not always
seem to have recognized.[44] The very argument that the sun
and its radiance were one light bordered on the position
that Father, Son, and Holy Spirit were no more than the
three modes of divine self-disclosure. But when Athanasius,
a generation after Nicaea, addressed himself to the doctrine
of the Holy Spirit, he showed his ability to deal with this
issue when it arose, employing the image of light and radiance to prove both the unity of the Son with the Spirit and
the unity of the Father with the Son.[45] Later in the fourth
century other fathers made use of the image of light and
radiance to reformulate the doctrine of the Trinity. Together with other images it was responsible for the idea that
the three persons of the Trinity were truly distinct, and

yet that each of them "coinhered" in the others.[46] This notion of "coinherence" provided a conceptual device missing in Athanasius. By means of this device the twin motifs identified at the beginning of this chapter as derivation and identity could finally achieve simultaneous expression. And through this notion the image of light went beyond its Athanasian use for the doctrine of the person of Christ and contributed to the formulation of the orthodox doctrine of the Trinity.

The primary function of the image in Athanasius was to express the doctrine of Christ, not the doctrine of the Trinity. For this purpose it was well suited, despite the weaknesses just mentioned. It provided him with a method of asserting the point he never tired of making: that in Christ faith had to do with no one less than God himself, and that therefore the believer could say to Christ, "In thy light do we see light."

4 SALVATION AS ILLUMINATION

"IN THY LIGHT DO WE SEE LIGHT."
For Athanasius this was indeed a confession of faith in God as he had revealed himself in Jesus Christ the radiance to be the light of the world. But, like every confession of faith, it spoke both about the divine reality and about the receiving of the divine reality. "We see light" was a summary of the gift of salvation granted in Christ. Into God's darkling world Christ had come as the radiance of the Father, "for us men and for our salvation." Salvation and illumination were two related ways of speaking about this gift. Or, as an epigram in the pseudo-Athanasian *Larger Treatise on Faith* summarized, "salvation proceeds from the Savior,

just as illumination does from the light."[1] Wherever Athanasius spoke of illumination, he meant some aspect of salvation; and wherever his language turned to the images of salvation and of cleansing, the image of illumination helped to clarify what those images implied.

Perhaps the most dramatic instance of the role played by the image of light in the language of Athanasius about salvation was an incident in his influential book about the founder of Christian monasticism, *The Life of St. Antony*.[2] Antony had been assailed by demons of every description. Taking the shapes of wild beasts and of reptiles, the demons beat him until he collapsed to the ground. Although he was torn by pain and was groaning, Antony defied the demons to do their worst. Finally deliverance came from heaven. As Athanasius put it, "Antony looked up and saw as it were the roof opening and a beam of light coming down to him. The demons suddenly were gone, and the pain in his body ceased at once."[3] Arrayed against him were all the forces of darkness. Actually, according to Athanasius' doctrine, they had no authority or power. For darkness was nonbeing, possessing no reality of its own unless someone treated it as though it were real.[4] When Antony recognized this and named the forces of nonbeing as the unreality they were, the power of divine light prevailed over the darkness to grant salvation to Antony. Knowing the name of a demon was the usual way to overpower him, but in Christian literature there was this added technique: to recognize that the powers of darkness had no being and to say so "in the name of Jesus."[5] The acknowledgment of divine being was a way of rescue from the tyranny of the forces of darkness.

Such rescue was the chief content of the Christian message as Athanasius interpreted it. The greatness of Athanasius was his single-minded and undeviating conviction that Christianity was a religion of salvation, and his refusal, even and especially in the conflict over the person of Christ, to regard as theologically essential any notion that could not be closely related to the theme of salvation. Throughout the conflict over the person of Christ and his coequality with the Father, Athanasius concentrated upon the implication of these issues for the salvation accomplished in Christ, and he was not long put off by arguments that lacked such implications. Even historians and theologians who interpret the rise of the orthodox doctrines of the Trinity and of the person of Christ unsympathetically are obliged to concede these three points: the moral character of Athanasius; the thoroughly biblical stamp of his theological method; and his devotion to the gospel of salvation. Thus, for example, Edward Gibbon, no partisan of Nicene orthodoxy, declared:

> Amid the storms of persecution, the archbishop of Alexandria was patient of labour, jealous of fame, careless of safety; and although his mind was tainted by the contagion of fanaticism, Athanasius displayed a superiority of character and abilities which would have qualified him, far better than the degenerate sons of Constantine, for the government of a great monarchy.[6]

And Adolf Harnack recognized the centrality of salvation in the thought of Athanasius when he asserted that "the theology and Christology of Athanasius have their roots in the idea of redemption." Indeed, continued Harnack,

> . . . in none of his major writings did Athanasius fail to
> base his anti-Arian Christology on the idea of redemp-
> tion; and whenever he gives [this as the basis], one gets
> the feeling that he is citing his most telling argument.[7]

Prominent as it was in his theological language, the image
of light performed the function it rendered in the *Life of
St. Antony*: It represented the deliverance from darkness
accomplished in Christ and granted to the children of God
in time of need.

The image of light was especially well suited for that
service because, among all the images applied to the person of Christ, it was perhaps the most adaptable to the work
of Christ as well. Each of these images did speak both about
the person and about the work. Christ as the "Son of God"
restored men to the Father and made them "sons of God"
by adoption. Christ as the "Logos of God" spoke the will
and word of God to men and made them rational in a new
and better way. Christ as the wisdom of God endowed men
with deeper wisdom. Nevertheless, most of the images deal-
ing with the person of Christ did not speak as explicitly of
what Christ had done as they did of what Christ had been.
When Christ was called the light, however, this referred
to his status as "light from light" and the radiance of the
Father; but it referred likewise to his redemptive office as
the light of the world, who had brought illumination and
salvation. This reference to his redemptive office was un-
doubtedly the original intention of the image; and the application of the image to his status was the result of further
thought about what the image implied, as Chapter 3 has
shown. First it meant his office, and only later his status.

When Athanasius was challenged by the Arians to explain the words of the gospel, "All things have been delivered to me" (Luke 10:22), he found this distinction between the office of Christ and the status of Christ helpful. Dubious though the distinction has proven to be—for Jesus Christ was what he did, and his work was his person, as the very title "Christ" implied[8]—it did make it possible for Athanasius to propose an interpretation of this passage according to which all things had been delivered to Christ not according to his person as the Son of God but for the sake of his work as the Savior of the world. As Son of God he had already had all things, but they were "delivered" or handed over to him so that he might save them. In other words,

> Man was "delivered" to him—as to a physician, to heal the serpent's sting; as to life, to raise the dead; as to light, to illumine the darkness; and since he is the Logos, to renew [man's] rationality.[9]

For an exegesis of the troubling verse from the gospels this was finally unsatisfactory, as Athanasius was to learn later on, when he felt constrained to revise his earlier exegesis and to apply the passage to the person of Christ after all.[10] Yet this exegesis does show how central the image of Christ as the light was to the thought and language of Athanasius about salvation. The incarnation of the Logos meant the renewal of the earth, the conquest of hell, and the victory of light over darkness.

That victory was accomplished through the incarnation, said Athanasius in his later thought about the matter, because by the incarnation man had become the recipient of all that the Son of God had previously been in relation to the Father. As the Logos and the radiance of the Father, he communicated all of this to men by becoming man himself, so that when he sanctified the human body, it was his own body that was sanctified.[11] Radiance of the Father he had always been, for God had never been "rayless."[12] Now, by the incarnation, the radiance of the Father irradiated the humanity he had assumed. As the principle and agent of creation, Christ was always the light of the world and of men; but as the Savior, whose cross meant "the healing of creation," he had become the light of the world, to illumine every man who came into the world.[13] So pervasive was this illumination, Athanasius asserted, that anyone who refused to accept Christ was as silly as a man who denied the existence of the sun when it was behind a cloud and yet wondered where all the light had come from. The power of the incarnation and of the cross had filled the whole world, as the light of the sun illumined the whole world even when the sun itself remained hidden.[14]

This analogy could be extended at least one step further. It was silly to deny the existence of the sun merely because it was hidden by a cloud, for its light filled the world. But even if one were blind and could not see the light of the sun, one would be silly to deny its existence; for the warmth of the sun was as pervasive as its light, and even a blind man perceived the heat of the sun. So also those who denied the light of the world could, according to Athanasius, perceive its warmth as this appeared in the lives of believers, and from this warmth they could acknowledge the power of Christ's resurrection.[15] This extension of the image had a significant role in the ethics of Athanasius, as Chapter 5 will show;[16] for it drew a direct line from the person and work of Christ to the life of the church. But the ground of this ethical judgment was the conviction of Athanasius that by his incarnation and resurrection Christ, the radiance of the Father, had brought a new being and a new power—new light and new warmth—into God's darkling world, transforming it so radically that only a blind man could fail to notice the light and that even he ought to be able to feel the warmth. As the Fourth Gospel expressed it, "And this is the judgment, that the light has come into the world, and men loved darkness rather than light, because their deeds were evil" (John 3:19).

To many whose thought had been molded by Greek patterns, the idea of the incarnation of the Logos for the salvation of man was repugnant because it seemed to be a desecration of the Holy. Behind the objections of many supporters of Arianism was the feeling that if the Logos were coequal with God, the incarnation of the Logos would be equivalent to a lese majesty. The image of Christ as the light provided Athanasius with a weapon to counter also this threat to the doctrine of salvation. The salvation of man by the incarnation of the Logos was not unworthy of the deity. Although Christ the light had come into the world, this did not mean that the world had bent the light into conformity with its shape or had extinguished the light by its darkness. Quite the reverse was the direction of the power. For when the rays of the sun illumined the earth, this illumination did not pollute the sun or exhaust its light.

Rather, the illumination brought salvation to the earth by driving out its darkness and purging its evil. In the same way the incarnation of the light did not identify him with the world in the sense that he was deprived of his nature; but by illumining the world with his beams, he brought purity to the body and sanctified it. Thus salvation as illumination did not pollute the light, but dispelled the darkness; the radiance of the Father did not exhaust his light, but cleansed the flesh.[17]

Probably the most controversial term for salvation in the language of Athanasius and other Greek fathers was not illumination but deification.[18] "He became human so that we might become divine" was his axiom about the meaning of salvation.[19] Few statements from the writings of Athanasius are quoted more often than this axiom, which usually appears as proof that the doctrine of salvation in Athanasius and in the Greek fathers was "physical" and that the content of salvation was not the forgiveness of sins, but the metaphysical transformation of man into God. Recently the controversy over the propriety of such language has broken out anew.[20] Although formulations of this sort were more frequent in the Eastern tradition of Christian thought than in the Western, Western theology and spirituality spoke in such language also; so, for that matter, did the Reformers and other Protestant divines. Nevertheless, "deification" does have an alien sound to most modern ears.

What did Athanasius mean by "deification"?[21] The image of Christ as the light may help to make his meaning precise, especially in combination with the concept of Christ as the Son of God. Both these images represented three principles which we can discern as governing the meaning of deification in the thought of Athanasius: first, the reality of the transformation in man that had been accomplished by the salvation given in Christ; second, the analogy between this transformation and the eternal status of Jesus Christ in relation to God; third, the unbridgeable ontological difference between the status of Christ and that of transformed humanity. Unless all three of these principles regulate the historical and theological interpretation of the idea of deification in Athanasius, the result will be a grave distortion of his thought. In his conflict with Arianism Athanasius was obliged to rethink the precise relation between the status of Christ and the status of the new humanity and to re-examine the specific relevance of the various biblical images for this issue. Only in the context of that re-examination of images does it become evident how the mature thought of Athanasius refined and defined the meaning of salvation as deification.

The salvation wrought by the incarnation of the Logos had effected a genuine transformation in man and in the world. The transformation was as genuine and as complete as the rout of darkness by light when the sun rose. Whatever darkness remained was dispelled by the coming of the light; "so also, now that the divine epiphany of the Logos of God has come, the darkness of the idols has no more power, but every part of the universe everywhere is being illumined by his doctrine."[22] The victory of darkness over light at sunrise was no illusion, but was objectively true. Its objective truth did not depend upon whether men acknowledged it or not. There would always be some who would deliberately turn away from the sunlight and wander about in dark places, seeing what was not there and not seeing what was there. So also men turned away from God and lived in the darkness of their own mistaken notions, imagining what was not true. But this did not negate the transformation that had been accomplished by the incarnation of the Logos.[23] In the remarkable denunciation of paganism that Athanasius put into the mouth of the uneducated monk Antony, this transformation became the ground for the question: "Was there ever a time when the knowledge of God shone so brightly?"[24] The idea of deification was a graphic way of saying that this change had penetrated the very nature of man and the structures of the world, making it possible for those who had been children of darkness and worshipers of demonic deities to become children of God. In fact, "by participation in the Son himself, we are said to participate in God."[25]

Because Christ was the light that enlightened every man who came into the world, the new status of the children of light was directly analogous to his status. Faced though Athanasius was by the Arian effort to close the gap between the status of Christ the light and the status of the children of light, he did not go to the other extreme. Thus he was not afraid to express the analogy between Christ and the Christian in the strongest of terms:

> Because of our relationship to his body we too have become the temple of God and therefore are made the sons of God. Thus even in us the Lord is now worshiped; and, as the apostle says [1 Cor. 14:25], those who see declare that the Lord is truly present in them.

. . . Truly he has received nothing from us for his own improvement, for the Logos of God has fullness and is without need. But it was we who were improved by him; for he is "the true light that enlightens every man coming into the world" [John 1:9].[26]

Once more it was the image of the light that expressed the analogy. As Christ was the true light that enlightened every man, the enlightened man shone with the true light and deserved to be called a son of God and a sharer in the nature of God. No merely intellectual or moral or symbolic transformation would do justice to the new being in Christ, nor therefore to the new creation accomplished by his incarnation, cross, and resurrection. Thus Athanasius concluded that Christ had become human so that men might become divine; such language was not too strong for the close analogy that Athanasius drew between the Son of God and the sons of God.

Despite the analogy, however, the difference between the being of the Logos and the being of those who had been transformed by his incarnation remained fundamental and unbridgeable. The incarnation had not altered the Holy Trinity. For the substantiation of this third principle, too, Athanasius turned to the image of light. The Son of God was by his very nature the Logos and the radiance of the Father. As such, he required no mediator between himself and the Father, but was the Logos and radiance directly and essentially. "But without the Spirit," Athanasius said by contrast, "we are alien and separate from God, and [only] by the participation of the Spirit are we knit [*synaptometha*] into the deity."[27] As a result, the being that men had in the Father was not their own being, a being of itself, but a being by virtue of the indwelling Spirit. There was an analogy of being between the divine light and the human lights, expressed by terms like "deification" and "the children of the light." But the analogy of being did not mean the identity of being. Similarly, both the Logos and creatures were called the "image of God"; but creatures were such an image by participation, while the Logos was the image of God by nature.[28] The children of God could even be said to participate in divine election before their historical existence, but this participation was fundamentally different from the pre-existence of the Logos and was indeed dependent upon it. Only if the Logos pre-existed eternally with God could the election of men be assured; for they were prefigured [*protetypōmenoi*] in him.[29]

The salvation and illumination of the world had come about through the incarnation; but if it was to reach those that dwelt in the shadows, it had to be disseminated. As a metaphor for this dissemination, the image of light once more provided Athanasius with a way of speaking that was simultaneously precise and dramatic. Light had a source at a particular time and place, but from this time and place it spread elsewhere to bring warmth and illumination. Whenever Athanasius spoke about the enlightenment of the world through the incarnation of the Logos, he was referring at the same time to the light of the gospel, by means of which Christ the light enlightened every man who came into the world. The message of the gospel had left the confines of Jerusalem and Judea and sent forth its rays throughout the world. On the basis of this mission and ex-

pansion of Christianity Athanasius sought to argue for the
correctness of orthodox teaching in contrast with heresy.
He demonstrated the presence and power of the light on
the ground of the illumination that had been spread to all
men everywhere.[30] The light of Judaism, he argued, had
been hidden under a bushel; but true teaching was distinguished from false teaching by the willingness of its
supporters to let their light shine. So it was that through
the gospel the light had become universal in its appeal and
influence:

> If Gentiles forsake their false religion and find refuge in
> the God of Abraham through the Logos, our Lord Jesus
> Christ [or: through the word of our Lord Jesus Christ],
> then it must be evident even to the most obstinate that
> the Christ has come, and that with his light he has il-
> lumined simply everyone, setting forth the true and
> divine doctrine about his Father.[31]

The transmission of light from its source into the darkness was an apt image for the spread of the gospel. It was
also a fitting metaphor for the personal appropriation of the
salvation accomplished in Christ. Previously lost in the
darkness, a man was illumined with salvation. According to
early Christian theologians, that happened in baptism; therefore one should not be surprised to find baptism referred to
as "illumination" in their writings.[32] As he argued his case
against Arianism, Athanasius turned his attention to the
subject of baptism, by which salvation and illumination
came from the Father through Christ to the believer. Baptism joined one to Christ and, through him, to the Father,
as the Trinitarian baptismal formula made clear.[33] The

baptism of Christ, like his anointing, was for the sake of others, not for his own; therefore when he was baptized, "we it is who are baptized in him."[34] So the illumination that came through baptism helped to substantiate Athanasius' doctrine that Christ the radiance was one with God the light.

In an extended argument Athanasius asserted this connection between the doctrine of baptism and the doctrine of the Trinity:

> Since the course of the discussion has led us also to refer to holy baptism, it is necessary to state what I think and believe: that when the Son is named together with the Father, this is not as if the Father were not all-sufficient; nor is it without meaning, and by accident. But since he is God's word and own wisdom, and is ever with the Father as his radiance, it is impossible, if the Father bestows grace, that he should not give it in the Son; for the Son is in the Father as the radiance in the light. . . . When baptism is given, whom the Father baptizes, him the Son baptizes; and whom the Son baptizes, he is consecrated in the Holy Spirit. And again, when the sun shines, one might say that the radiance illuminates; for the light is one and indivisible, and it cannot be detached [from the radiance]. In the same way, where the Father is or is named, there plainly the Son is also. Is the Father named in baptism? Then the Son must be named with him.[35]

Thus the illumination that came by means of baptism was the appropriation of the illumination sent forth by Christ as the radiance of the Father.

The image of the light helped to explain almost every

motif in the thought of Athanasius. No other language
about the divine reality, not even the idea of God as the
Father or of Christ as the Logos and the Son of God,
adapted itself so plastically to the doctrine of God, the
meaning of revelation, the relation of Christ to God, the
new being in Christ, and, as Chapter 5 shows, the new life
of the church as it participated in that new being. Each of
these perennial Christian issues was given fresh meaning
and power as it took the form of another variation on the
theme of Christ the light of the world. On the other hand,
this theme created certain difficulties in Athanasius' treatment of each of these issues, as we have seen in previous
chapters. The description of salvation as illumination en-
countered such difficulties also. Even in the thought of a
theologian who was as saturated in the Scriptures as Athanasius the impression was almost unavoidable that the enlightenment given in salvation applied primarily to the mind
and the intellect.

Thus Athanasius could speak about having the mind illumined or about having "the eyes of the mind [*dianoia*]
disabled."[36] In his early apologetic he attributed heresy to
the darkening of the soul, which closed its eyes and therefore could not see the light of divine truth.[37] Created for
the vision of God and for illumination by God, the soul
looked at evil instead and was deluded into seeing it as real.
These and similar turns of phrase in Athanasius can lend
support to the charge that he intellectualized faith into a
species of knowledge, a charge that has sometimes been
leveled at him and at other Greek fathers. Despite these
turns of phrase, however, a fair study of the image of il-

lumination in Athanasius does not uphold the charge. When he spoke of the darkness in the human mind, as in the passage just cited, he almost always included explicit mention of the perversity in the human will. When he described the illumination of man by the coming of the gospel, he did indeed refer to the new knowledge of God that had come through the incarnation; but such a description almost never failed to speak also of the new courage, peace, and moral resolve that were the gift of faith. When Athanasius set out to specify the content of the Christian message, his vocation as a defender of Nicene orthodoxy against the Arians compelled him to dwell upon the doctrinal and even propositional aspects of the message. But even in the midst of his vigorous polemics against Arianism or of his arguments in favor of the orthodox interpretation of the Scriptures, the existential character of the Christian message as a message of salvation continued to make its presence felt.

As a message of salvation, the gospel brought illumination to the total life of man—not to his intellect only, to be sure, but to his intellect also. Christ was the bringer of a new creation, which had transformed the old order and had established the victory of light over darkness. As the Logos, the Word and Reason of God, he had put darkness and irrationality to flight. But he had not come as the founder of a new philosophical school, offering to exchange a new set of abstract ideas for the old. The salvation he had brought was "the healing of creation."[38] Against Arianism Athanasius contended as fiercely as he did for the total coequality of Christ with the Father, not because this was a correct idea intellectually, but because it was a necessary idea religiously. Athanasius was not a bold or speculative mind. As F. L. Cross has said,

> Those who looked for the daring of an Origen, the learning of a Eusebius, the polemics of a Jerome, or the culture of a Gregory of Nazianzum, would have sought for such qualities in Athanasius in vain.[39]

It was not from a concern for knowledge, but from a concern for salvation that he argued. An illumination that was mental did not require the personal presence of God in the history of Jesus Christ. Moses and the prophets could have brought such an illumination. But God had to come personally in Jesus Christ to achieve an illumination that broke the power of darkness and dispelled its tyranny over the world. No lesser force could have accomplished this, and from the illumination that had in fact come Athanasius argued for the full deity of the one who had brought it.

So it was that "salvation proceeds from the Savior, just as illumination does from the light." The cleansing power of the light had penetrated the darkness in the coming of Christ. Those who had received it and had been cleansed by it no longer lived in the darkness, but had become "children of the light," as Chapter 5 will show. They knew what Christ was because they experienced what Christ did in them and to them. The illumination in which they now lived showed that the radiance had shone in them. And the radiance, in turn, pointed beyond itself to the light with which it was one. As the church contemplated what the light had brought and as it worshiped the source of its own being, its illumination reflected his light. The church viewed itself and its world differently because the illumination had come in Christ. It viewed God differently too, because his personal radiance had brought the illumination that transformed and healed every human vision. The gift of this salvation, accomplished by God the light in Christ the radiance, Athanasius found represented in the image of the light, as confessed by the psalmist: "In thy light do we see light."

5 CHILDREN OF THE LIGHT

meant to Athanasius that the light of God, which had shone forth in Jesus Christ, had penetrated the darkness of the world and had transformed men by bringing them salvation. This transformation was a reality, not merely a phrase. The coming of the light did make a difference. As surely as Christ was the radiance of the Father and the light of the world, not according to the imagination of believers but according to truth, so surely those who now believed and obeyed him as the light were the children of the light. Once more it was a pseudonymous treatise that best summarized the teaching of Athanasius: "As long as he was upon earth according to the incarnation, he was light in the world, as he said himself [John 12:36], 'While you have light, believe in the light, that you may be the children of light.' "[1]

For their status as the children of the light men were dependent upon Christ in his status as light and radiance, for they participated in the light that he radiated. The mature reflection of Athanasius developed this insight into an almost full-blown Trinitarian principle:

> As then the Father is light and the Son is his radiance . . . we may see in the Son the Spirit also by whom we are enlightened. "That he may give you," it says [Eph. 1:17], "the Spirit of wisdom and of revelation in the knowledge of him, having the eyes of your hearts enlightened." But when we are enlightened by the Spirit, it is Christ who in him enlightens us. For it says [John 1:9]: "There was the true light which enlightens every man coming into the world."[2]

The illumination and salvation accomplished by his coming into the flesh were transmitted and communicated to the newly enlightened by the enlightening Spirit. But as Athanasius argued, against the deniers of the coequality of the Son, that the radiance and the light had to be one; so he argued, against those who contravened the coequality of the Spirit, that the light communicated by the Spirit had to be identical with that shed abroad by the radiance, which was, in turn, the very light of the Father.[3] Saying that the Spirit enlightened was another way of expressing the axiom that whatever enlightenment there was in the world had come from the Son of God.

Dependent as they were upon Christ the radiance for

their status as children of the light, men had a share in him
as he had a share in them. A failure to understand this
reciprocity between Christ the radiance and the children of
the light caused the Arians to conclude from the weakness
of Christ in his flesh that there was little or no difference between Christ and other men.[4] Yet it was not in an
attack upon the Arians, but in a treatise written in 357 to
defend his own flight from persecution, that Athanasius
penned the most pithy summary of this reciprocity. He was
citing the example of Jesus in the gospels to prove that
under certain circumstances it was legitimate for believers
to withdraw and hide rather than to face their persecutors.
Certainly, he declared, no one would be so audacious as to
charge the Lord with cowardice. But what the Lord had
done was not for his own sake but for the sake of believers.

> For whatever is written concerning our Savior in his
> human nature, ought to be considered as applying to the
> whole race of mankind; because he took our body, and
> exhibited in himself human infirmity.[5]

Flight to avoid persecution could therefore be as lawful for
believers as it was for Christ. He did not need to flee. He
was, after all, the light that enlightened every man coming
into the world. No human darkness could ever have extinguished his light. Yet for the salvation and comfort of
the children of the light he had hidden himself from his
tormentors.

Even for their weakness and need, therefore, the children
of the light showed their dependence upon Christ the radiance. Much more did they depend upon him for their light

and strength. Of themselves they did not have the power or the right to come to God, but on their accounts Christ had been made the way and door to God. When they shared in the knowledge of the Father which he communicated and were enlightened and cleansed by him, they gained the purity of heart that was the one prerequisite to the vision of God. "Blessed," Athanasius quoted from Psalm 119:1, "are the undefiled in the way," which meant in Christ, who was the way; and from Matthew 5:8 he quoted the parallel benediction: "Blessed are the pure in heart, for they shall see God."[6] To Athanasius the primary meaning of this beatitude was not, as it has been for many, that "the initiative lies with the one who seeks to see" or that men by their penances or piety could render themselves worthy of the vision of God, but that in Christ God had given men the way, the purity, and therefore the vision.[7] This beatitude was therefore a paraphrase of the theme from the Psalms: "In thy light do we see light." For Christ the light and radiance granted men a pure heart, and in this light they were able to see God the light.

This emphasis upon enlightenment as a gift from God rather than as an achievement of man was not so ethically impotent in Athanasius as it has sometimes become in those who have stressed the priority of the divine initiative. For although it was certain that the moral striving of man did not accomplish purity and the vision of God, membership in the community of those who shared that vision did have certain prerequisites. He who wanted to have a part in the communion of the saints had to begin to imitate the life of the saints. In support of this insistence upon moral purification Athanasius cited the analogy of vision and light. Anyone who wanted to see the light of the sun, he wrote, would cleanse and wipe his eye, until it itself became light in some sense; for vision was contingent upon purity. In the same way anyone who wanted to understand the light of the Scriptures and to be associated with those who understood what the Scriptures meant would naturally want to bring the pattern of his life into conformity with theirs; otherwise he could not possibly understand what God had revealed to them.[8] What no unaided eye had seen, that God had disclosed to the pure in heart.

But when Athanasius began to specify the precise content of the moral purity prerequisite to the vision of God, his description gave the impression that the text of the beatitude, "Blessed are the pure in heart, for they shall see God," was the basis for a life of asceticism.[9] He seems to have identified true purity in heart with a withdrawal from society. Evidence to support this misgiving about what it meant to be a child of the light comes from Athanasius' *The Life of St. Antony*. There Athanasius set forth the life story of a true "gymnast for God," whose strenuous denial of himself and of the world won for him the gift of the vision of God. From the warm admiration of the biographer for his subject it appears that Athanasius regarded this life as the true realization of the Christian ideal. The biography was aimed at pagan readers too, as proof that true Christians could trample the demons underfoot.[10] Athanasius filled the book with accounts of how Antony, by his counsel and example, strengthened the Christian faith and life of people who lived out in the world among men.[11]

Yet Antony's own vocation lay in separation from the world. As Athanasius said of him,

> Antony had to do only with prayer and the practice of asceticism, for the sake of which he lived his mountain life, happy in the contemplation of the divine and grieving that many disturbed him and forced him to the outer mountain.[12]

When Antony did touch ordinary society for a moment in order to give advice or help, this was a concession on his part to the way most people had to live.

It is difficult to escape the impression that according to Antony, and for that matter according to Athanasius, this angelic life was preferable to one lived amid the moral ambiguities of civil society. The Anthanasius who, as a young man, saw the church and the empire come to terms, also saw the church and the world beginning to come to terms. It was easier to be a member of the church than it had been during the third century. Even the persecution of orthodox bishops by Arian emperors, indeed, even the reign of the emperor Julian, did not cut off the steady growth of the church in both size and prestige. Ironically, the more children of the light there were, the dimmer their light sometimes seemed. The moral rigor of an Antony seemed to be one way out of this problem, and it was the way followed by much of the church since: a double standard of Christian morality, by which the professional religious were thought to live up to the highest demands of the divine law, while the ordinary folk of the church were not expected to obey its sterner requirements. Thus even the Christian emperor needed the intercession of the hermit.[13]

Christian emperors and other believers were children of light too, but their light often flickered and almost went out. The truly incandescent light came from the monks.

As we have seen at the beginning of this chapter, the children of the light had their light from Christ the radiance. If the monks were children of the light with a particular brilliance, they must have come closer to Christ in the quality of their lives than the average believers did. There were, in fact, notable parallels between Athanasius' account of the life of Antony and Athanasius' conception of the earthly life of Jesus.[14] The honorific title *Christophoros*, "Christbearer," was applied to an ascetic, the nun Polycratia, whose excesses of fasting and self-denial had thoroughly debilitated her body.[15] In the vocabulary that Athanasius employed in praise of St. Antony appeared some of the same words and phrases that he applied to the person of Christ elsewhere. For example, Athanasius said of Antony:

> It was not his stature or figure that made him stand out from the rest, but his settled character and the purity of his soul. For his soul was imperturbed, and so his outward appearance was calm.[16]

This "gift from the Savior" had its counterpart in the picture of the Savior as one who, while impassible himself, granted aid and comfort to others in their suffering. As a modern editor of *The Life of St. Antony* points out, commenting upon this passage,

> Antony, in other words, possessed in a very high degree Christian *apatheia*—perfect self-control, freedom from

passion—the ideal of every true monk and ascetic striving for perfection. Christ, who was free from every emotional weakness and fault—*apathēs Christos*—is his model.[17]

This judgment could perhaps be inverted to read that to some extent Athanasius conformed his portrait of Christ to the monastic definition of the blessed life.

In *The Life of St. Antony* Athanasius described another characteristic of the Christian life, a characteristic grounded in the image of light and vision. When Antony gave an account of the content of the Christian life and of Christian faith, he spoke of "rejoicing in the Lord, meditating on the good things to come and contemplating the things that are the Lord's, considering that everything is in the Lord's hands."[18] If salvation meant illumination, the life of the saved found its focus in the contemplation of God and of divine things. It was consistent with this emphasis when Athanasius defined the fall of man as a lapse from the contemplation of God and the things of God to the contemplation of the body. The statement of Genesis 3:7 that "they knew that they were naked" was taken to mean that Adam and Eve diverted their gaze from Creator to creature in the lust of narcissism.[19] Hence sin meant the contemplation of corruptible things and of darkness, in default of the vision of God. Both this description of the contemplative life and its very vocabulary betrayed the Greek ancestry of these ideas. Despite the occasional references to "seeing God" in the Old Testament and the New, the contemplative ideal was not the form in which the prophets usually couched their understanding of the good life. Hearing and therefore obeying, rather than seeing and contemplating, were the principal organs of faith in the Hebraic tradition.

If God was light and if Christ was the radiance of the Father, illumination was a legitimate way to describe salvation, and vision or contemplation was an appropriate image for the life of the children of the light. Unlike most language for the Christian life, the image of vision and contemplation succeeded in making clear the direct and immediate continuity between the saving action of God and the new reality of the life in God. Not even a phrase like "action and response" would do as much justice to the immediacy and spontaneity of the Christian ethic as did Athanasius' picture of God the light shedding his illumination through Christ the radiance and thus granting men the vision of his glory. For this accent in the ethic of Athanasius few images would have been as satisfactory. But the image of light and vision tended to break down at the point of the disjunction between the contemplative life and the active life in the theoretical ethics of classical antiquity. An ethic that was oriented principally to this image found the contemplative life of Christian meditation easier to describe than the active life of Christian obedience, and it ran the danger of seeing in monasticism the exemplar for all Christian living. As the image of Christ as radiance was incomplete without other images like Logos and Son of God, so the definition of the Christian life as "the contemplation of the things that are the Lord's" needed to be supplemented by more dynamic and more existential ways of speaking about the new life of the children of the light.

Perhaps the most existential way of speaking about the new life in Athanasius was his emphasis upon the Christian victory over the fear of death.[20] Here the picture of the Christian life as the life of light proved that it did not have to issue in quietism. As he set about demonstrating the superiority of Christianity to both paganism and Judaism, Athanasius was reminded of the courage of the Christian martyrs during the persecutions so recently ended.[21] This he contrasted with the fear of death not only in Greek and Roman paganism, but even in the Old Testament. It was not correct, he said, to chide those who were afraid of death; for being made out of nothing and therefore living under the shadow of nonbeing, man continually faced the prospect of fading back into the darkness out of which he had come. The fear of death was thus an eloquent testimony to the creation of man. If creation meant that man could "be" only by the power of the "God-who-is," the fear of death was the fear of losing one's hold on this power of being. This fear turned even the brave into cowards; when it struck, men wept as though the dead had perished. So slender a hold did man have on being that the threat of nonbeing hung over him and filled him with terror.[22] Therefore the devil rejoiced in death because of the power it gave him over men.

The incarnation of the Logos and his death on the cross had changed all that. Now not only mature and strong men, but even youths and young maidens manifested in fact that contempt for death which classical philosophy had claimed in theory. The natural attitude toward death was to fear it, but now men had learned to live from resources that transcended the merely natural and therefore to greet death and even martyrdom as a manifestation of the will of God. By nature men were frail and afraid of the corruption that death brought in its wake. But something had happened to deliver them from this weakness and fear and to give them a strength and courage not of their own making. That something was the incarnation and death, and particularly the resurrection, of Christ. Only if death itself had died as a result of his coming, was it possible to explain how mere men could despise death as they did. They treated death as nonexistent because the resurrection of Christ had proved that it was nonexistent, just as his power over demons had shown that they belonged to the realm of nonbeing. No dead man could continue to exert such power over death, over demons, and over idols. Only one who had himself triumphed over death could be so powerful in his war against death. Paganism had not produced martyrs; but now plain people, not merely saints and heroes, died with joy and prayer on their lips.

This idealized picture was intended to prove that something fundamentally different had happened through the coming of Christ. Athanasius summarized the Christian attitude toward the prospect of death in an epigram he attributed to St. Antony: "When we awaken each day, we should think that we shall not live till evening; and again, when about to go to sleep, we should think that we shall not awaken."[23] This cavalier treatment of "the last enemy" was due, he said, not to an extra measure of heroism in Christians, but to the courage that came from Christ. If heroes had regarded death this way, that would perhaps have shown how heroic they were. But if men who were frail could manifest such contempt for death,

Athanasius maintained that the explanation had to be sought in something beyond mere heroism. As he pondered the meaning of this transformation, he drew once more upon the image of darkness and light:

> After the night the sun rises, and the entire territory of the earth is illumined by it. Then there can be no doubt that it is the sun which has diffused its light everywhere, both dispelling the darkness and illumining everything. So now, since the saving epiphany of the Savior in flesh and his death on the cross, death is despised and trodden underfoot; from this it must be obvious that it is the Savior himself who has appeared in the body, destroyed death, and manifested in his own disciples the daily marks of his victory over [death].[24]

When a landscape that was not luminous of itself began to light up, Athanasius continued in the same imagery, that was a sign of some light from beyond; thus also the illumination of human life even in the face of death reflected a light whose origin was more than human. For even a blind man could recognize the presence of the sun from the warmth it dispersed, though he could not see its light. In the same way even those who did not acknowledge the truth of the Christian message of the incarnation had to admit, from the warmth of the Christian light they had witnessed, that a new and radical transformation had taken place.[25] The contempt for death and the courage in its presence that marked the Christian life were a light whose warmth even the blindness of unbelief was compelled to admit. The children of the light did not exhaust the meaning of the light in contemplation and meditation, but the light transformed their entire outlook on both life and death. In the light of the resurrection of Christ they could see the light of their own lives, because the illumination that was salvation meant the end of the reign of darkness. Those who had dwelt in the shadow of death had discovered the light of new life in Christ, whose light and warmth were reflected in their faith and courage.

From this faith and courage the children of the light received a new tranquillity. The sight of demonic forces, said the sermon of Antony, produced a turbulence in the human soul, but the vision of the angels produced joy, gladness, and courage.[26] For the angels did not come of their own accord, but the joy of the Lord and the power of God the Father were with them. Therefore the soul had its judgment illumined by the radiance of the Father. Enlightened with these rays, it looked at the spirits that appeared and discerned that they were good. Thus salvation illumined not only the individual soul in itself, but the whole world of things visible and invisible. Released from darkness by the coming of the light, the children of the light did not need to fear the power of the demonic darkness. For this new peace and for the new discernment it brought, Athanasius could find no image more apt than the metaphor of light prevailing over darkness.

The same image performed yet another service in the ethics of Athanasius. As in the Sermon on the Mount (Matt. 5:16), it described for him the influence of the Christian life upon those who did not yet share its light. It was important, he warned, not to judge the children of the light by temporary outward appearances. In their outward appearance the children of the light were often obscure and unknown, as Antony had been in the desert. If they were to be judged by what men call light, they would be called darkness. But it was the way of God eventually to make known those who were his.

> For though they do their work in secret and though they wish to remain obscure, yet the Lord shows them forth as lamps to all men, that thus again those who hear of them may realize that the commandments can lead to perfection, and may take courage on the path to virtue.[27]

Thus Athanasius adapted the language of the Sermon on the Mount to say that God hid his lights under the bushel of obscurity until, in his own good time, he let their beams illumine the world. Then St. Antony, who had preferred the life of quiet meditation to the bustle of commerce or of politics, gained world-wide renown for his saintliness. As the light of God in Christ had broken forth when God caused it to shine, so the children of the light illumined the world at God's command.

This simple and almost homely metaphor for the Christian life took on a new and more profound significance in the context of the theological and Christological use of the image of light in the thought of Athanasius. The children of the light were the children of that light which had shone forth in Christ the radiance to grant the illumination of salvation to a darkling world. When Athanasius applied such language to the Christian ethic, therefore, he freighted it with all the theological and metaphysical connotations we have been reviewing in this study. Darkness stood for sin, not merely as a moral evil, but as the threat of nonbeing. The new life was the life of light, not merely as moral virtue, but as a participation in the power of God the light. And those who had been translated from darkness to light had not merely acquired new rules for living; when they were brought out into the light, their very being had been rescued from the terror of annihilation. To be children of the light and to shine as lamps meant to be the channels through which the power of being delivered and sustained the world.

In keeping with this interpretation of the children of the light, Athanasius concluded that no one less than God himself—no creature, not even an angel—was present in the midst of the people of God. This conclusion was at issue in the controversy of his later years over the divinity of the Holy Spirit. Athanasius took his support from the statement of Deuteronomy 1:30: "The Lord your God who goes before you." He interpreted this statement to mean that the presence of God among his people was personal and direct, not mediated through some creature. And since God was Father, Son, and Holy Spirit, the presence of God was the presence of the holy and undivided Trinity. "Thus the Spirit of God is neither angel nor creature, but belongs to his Godhead. For when the Spirit was with the people, God, through the Son in the Spirit, was with them."[28] So God dwelt with the church and in the church. The church was composed of children of the light because God was the light.[29] What radiated from the church to illumine the world was, in this ultimate sense, nothing less than the uncreated light that was God. The modern dichotomy between theology and ethics does

justice neither to the way Athanasius spoke about faith
and life nor to the deepest significance of the key images,
like that of light, which served both his theology and his
ethics. Even though the scriptural instances of the image
may not actually connote all of this each time, Athanasius
employed an exegesis in which the rhetorical admonitions
of the Scriptures acquired a more profound significance
through their association with these key images.

Thus when Antony admonished, in the language of 2
Corinthians 6:14, that "there simply is no fellowship of light
with darkness" and that therefore orthodox Christians were
to avoid any contact with the Arians,[30] Athanasius may
well have read this admonition as a practical application of
his teaching about Christ as the radiance of God. The true
believers were "light" and the false believers "darkness,"
because the true believers accepted the light of God as it
had come in Christ. Children of this light could not have
anything to do with darkness because darkness was nonbeing. By the same exegetical method Athanasius contrasted the death of Christ with that of Isaiah or John the
Baptist, declaring that Christ had been neither beheaded
nor sawn in half, to avoid giving any justification to those
who would like to divide the church.[31] Clearly the image of
the church as the body of Christ was a *paradeigma* to Athanasius. It said something about both Christ and the church
that was really so in their very nature. So, too, the image
of light and darkness revealed the nature of both the
Creator and the creature.

Over the darkling world the demonic powers had drawn
a veil, to keep men from realizing that this was still God's

world. But God had pierced the veil by coming in Christ, who was "light from light" and the very radiance of the Father. By him God had saved and illumined his darkling world, "to give light to those who sit in darkness and in the shadow of death." (Luke 1:79). All of this, and more, was the meaning of the "the light of the world" to Athanasius. It would appear to have been the meaning of "light" to an even earlier and even greater Christian theologian, who wrote, as if to summarize all the Athanasian themes:

> And even if our gospel is veiled, it is veiled only to those who are perishing. In their case the god of this world has blinded the minds of the unbelievers, to keep them from seeing the light of the gospel of the glory of Christ, who is the likeness of God. For what we preach is not ourselves, but Jesus Christ as Lord, with ourselves as your servants for Jesus' sake. For it is the God who said, "Let light shine out of darkness," who has shone in our hearts to give the light of the knowledge of the glory of God in the face of Christ (2 Cor. 4:3-6).

Or, in the words of the psalm, "in thy light do we see light."

NOTES

INTRODUCTION

1. Martin Luther, *Lectures on Genesis,* ed. Jaroslav Pelikan, *Luther's Works,* 2 (St. Louis, 1960), 247.
2. See, for example, Bertil Gärtner, *The Theology of the Gospel According to Thomas,* trans. Eric J. Sharpe (New York, 1961), pp. 144-149; R. M. Grant, *Gnosticism and Early Christianity* (New York, 1959), pp. 42-46.
3. James Henry Breasted, *Development of Religion and Thought in Ancient Egypt* (New York, 1912), pp. 8-17 and *passim.*
4. In the preface to his book *Die Sonne der Gerechtigkeit und der Schwarze* (Münster in Westfalen, 1918), Dölger traces his interest in this problem to the summer of 1912. See also his *Sol salutis* (Münster in Westfalen, 1925). The volumes of Dölger's private journal, *Antike und Christentum* (1929 ff.) contain many studies of the image of light and the sun both in early Christianity and in its background, and I shall be referring to these later in this book.
5. Franz-Norbert Klein, *Die Lichtterminologie bei Philon von Alexandrien und in den hermetischen Schriften* (Leiden, 1961) is to be an effort to compare and contrast Philo's use of the image of light with the usage in "Hermes Trismegistus."
6. Cf. Harold R. Willoughby, *Pagan Regeneration* (Chicago, 1929), p. 128.
7. Rudolf Bultmann, "Zur Geschichte der Lichtsymbolik im Altertum," *Philolologus,* XCVII (1948), 1-36.
8. Mircea Eliade, *Patterns in Comparative Religion,* trans. Rosemary Sheed (New York, 1958), p. 124; see also Prof. Eliade's extensive bibliography, pp. 152-153.
9. John Milton, *Paradise Lost,* Book III, lines 1 ff.
10. Paul Tillich, *Systematic Theology,* II (Chicago, 1957, 165.
11. The new Berlin edition of Athanasius, *Athanasius Werke,* edited by Hans-Georg Opitz *et al.* (Berlin, 1934 ff.) is, unfortunately, still very incomplete. I have been compelled, therefore, to rely primarily upon the old edition in J. P. Migne, *Patrologia, Series Graeca,* correcting Migne from the later edition wherever this was possible. I have also made use of various other editions of individual works, especially those in the superbly edited "Sources chrétiennes" series, and of the English translations of Newman, Robertson, Shapland, and Meyer. Most of the translations in the text, however, are my own, although I have consulted

(and borrowed from) earlier renditions into English. For the study of Athanasius' writings, three reference works are indispensable, and I have drawn upon all of them in the preparation of this book: on the state of the transmission of his works, Hans-Georg Opitz, *Untersuchungen zur Ueberlieferung der Schriften des Athanasius* (Berlin, 1935); on his vocabulary, Guido Müller, *Lexicon Athanasianum* (Berlin, 1952); and on works by him and about him, the bibliographies of Johannes Quasten, *Patrology*, III (Westminster, Md., 1960), 20-79. In my citation of Athanasius, I shall give the Latin title of the work, followed by the number of the book and paragraph, followed in turn by its location in the Migne edition (abbreviated as *MPG*). Since I have used the familiar 1857 edition of Migne, the pagination of the *De decretis* peculiar to that edition appears here as well.

1 GOD AS LIGHT

1. Origen *Contra Celsum*, VI, 61-64; cf. R. P. C. Hanson, *Allegory and Event* (London, 1959), pp. 220-221.

2. Origen, *op. cit.*, VII, 27. See also Henry Chadwick's comment on this latter passage in his edition of the *Contra Celsum* (Cambridge, 1953), p. 416.

3. Cf. the discussion of Gregory Dix, *Jew and Greek* (New York, 1953), pp. 76-83. See also p. 63 below.

4. *In illud, "Omnia mihi tradita, etc.,"* 3, *MPG* 25, 216.*

5. *Orationes contra Arianos*, II, 32, *MPG* 26, 216.

6. *Ibid.*, II, 36, *MPG* 26, 224.

7. Paul Tillich, *Theology of Culture* (New York, 1959), p. 59.

8. C. R. B. Shapland (ed.), *The Letters of Saint Athanasius Concerning the Holy Spirit* (London, 1951), pp. 133-134. See also *De synodis*, 6, *MPG* 26, 689; and the note of John Henry Newman (ed.), *Select Treatises of St. Athanasius in Controversy with the Arians* (2nd ed.; London, 1881), II, 311-315.

9. *Epistolae ad Serapionem*, I, 17, *MPG* 26, 569.

10. *Orationes contra Arianos*, III, 18, *MPG* 26, 360-361.

11. *Epistolae ad Serapionem*, I, 20, *MPG* 26, 577.

12. *De decretis Nicaenae synodi*, 24, *MPG* 25, 457.

13. Plato, *Republic*, IX, 592B. Cf. Werner Jaeger, *Paideia*, trans. Gilbert Highet, II (New York, 1943), 354-357.

14. Plato, *Parmenides*, 132D; see also Aristotle, *Metaphysics*, I, 991A.

15. *Oratio contra gentes*, 4, *MPG* 25, 9. On God as "he-who-is" cf. p. 33 below.

16. Guido Müller, *Lexicon Athanasianum* (Berlin, 1952), cols. 1094-1095, lists the instances of *paradeigma* in the writings of Athanasius. Perhaps the most extensive and important discussion of the *paradeigmata*, especially that of light and radiance, occurs in *De decretis Nicaenae synodi*, 23-24, *MPG* 25, 456-457.

* See note 11, p. 113, for explanation of reference abbreviation.

17. Jaroslav Pelikan, *Luther the Expositor* (St. Louis, 1959), pp. 23-27.

18. *De synodis*, 42, MPG 26, 768.

19. *De decretis Nicaenae synodi*, 12, MPG 25, 445.

20. Paul S. Minear, *Images of the Church in the New Testament* (Philadelphia, 1960), p. 221. Minear's entire first chapter is a provocative analysis of the problems with which Athanasius also dealt as he considered the meaning of the biblical *paradeigmata*. Cf. also Ernest Evans (ed.), *Tertullian's Treatise Against Praxeas* (London, 1948), p. 238.

21. See pp. 64 ff.

22. See pp. 69-70 below.

23. *De synodis*, 39, MPG 26, 761.

24. *Orationes contra Arianos*, III, 59, MPG 26, 445-448.

25. *Tomus ad Antiochenos*, 8, MPG 26, 805.

26. *De synodis*, 41, MPG 26, 765.

27. *De decretis Nicaenae synodi*, 23, MPG 25, 456.

28. G. L. Prestige, *God in Patristic Thought* (London, 1956), p. 214.

29. Cf. F. J. Dölger, "Lumen Christi," *Antike und Christentum*, V (1936), 1-43, esp. 11-26 on the *Phōs hilaron*.

30. Cf. Paul Tillich, *Systematic Theology*, I (Chicago, 1951), 238-241.

31. *Orationes contra Arianos*, I, 23, MPG 26, 60.

32. Karl Barth, *Church Dogmatics*, I-1, *The Doctrine of the Word of God*, trans. G. T. Thomson, (Edinburgh, 1936), 451, quoting this passage from Athanasius.

33. Cf. the argument in *Orationes contra Arianos*, III, 11, MPG 26, 344-345; see also the parallels assembled in Robertson's note *ad locum*.

34. *De decretis Nicaenae synodi*, 11, MPG 25, 441.

35. *Orationes contra Arianos*, III, 63, MPG 26, 456.

36. See, for example, Plato, *Republic*, X, 595-598; and *Timaeus*, 38A and 48E.

37. *Orationes contra Arianos*, III, 19-20, MPG 26, 364.

38. Cf. Wilhelm Michaelis in Gerhard Kittel (ed.) *Theologisches Wörterbuch zum Neuen Testament* (Stuttgart, 1933 ff.), IV, 661-678, esp. 663-665 on Platonic and related usage.

39. 1 John 1:5, so quoted in *Epistolae ad Serapionem*, I, 19, MPG 26, 573; it is quoted as "God is light" in *De decretis Nicaenae synodi*, 27, MPG 25, 465.

40. *Epistolae ad Serapionem*, I, 19, MPG 26, 573.

41. Werner Elert, *Der Ausgang der altkirchlichen Christologie* (Berlin, 1957), p. 74. The entire discussion, pp. 71-132, is an interpretation of how this axiom established itself as the a priori of both sides in the Monophysite controversies; on Athanasius, cf. pp. 79-81.

42. See the passages cited in Th. Camelot (ed.), *Contre les paiens et Sur l'incarnation du Verbe*, "Sources chrétiennes," 18 (Paris, 1957), 165, note 1.

43. *Oratio contra gentes*, 28, MPG 25, 56.

44. *Orationes contra Arianos*, I, 23, MPG 26, 60. The word I have

translated as "the very notion" is *ennoia;* the Euclidean term for "axioms" was *koinai ennoiai.*

45. *Oratio contra gentes,* 39, MPG 25, 77.

46. *Epistola ad Afros episcopos,* 7, MPG 26, 1041. Cf. T. E. Pollard, "The Impassibility of God," *Scottish Journal of Theology,* VIII (1955), 353-364.

47. Alfred North Whitehead, *Process and Reality* (New York, 1929), p. 526; the italics are his.

2 GOD'S DARKLING WORLD

1. There is a fine bibliography on the theological and philosophical significance of analogy in William F. Lynch, *Christ and Apollo. The Dimensions of the Literary Imagination* (New York, 1960), pp. 223-225. Father Lynch's discussion of "the analogical," *ibid.,* pp. 133-160, while not directly related to the issue I am discussing here, provides a helpful orientation to the general problem.

2. *Oratio contra gentes,* 1, MPG 25, 5.

3. *Orationes contra Arianos,* II, 21, MPG 26, 192.

4. *Ibid.* The distinction is developed at greater length in *De decretis Nicaenae synodi,* 11, MPG 25, 441-444.

5. *Orationes contra Arianos,* IV, 18-19, MPG 26, 493-496. The problem of the provenance of the *Fourth Discourse* is set forth at length and with much learning by A. Stegmann, *Die pseudoathanasianische "IVte Rede gegen die Arianer" als "kata Areianōn logos," ein Apollinarisgut* (Rottenberg, 1917).

6. On Athanasius' doctrine of creation and the fall cf. R. Bernard, *L'image de Dieu d'après saint Athanase* (Paris, 1952).

7. *Oratio contra gentes,* 8, MPG 25, 17.

8. *Ibid.,* 7, MPG 25, 16.

9. *Oratio de incarnatione Verbi,* 4, MPG 25, 104.

10. See p. 33 on God as *ho ōn.*

11. *Oratio de incarnatione Verbi,* 42, MPG 25, 169.

12. *Ibid.* See also 44, MPG 25, 176, on the Logos as "the life" in person.

13. The verb used here is *ousioō,* which appears in the works of Plotinus but occurs nowhere else in the writings of Athanasius. No single English verb would seem to suffice as a translation. To "reify" means to endow with being, but primarily in speech or in the imagination; nor does the English verb "realize," even if we overlook its corruption in American usage, convey the same meaning.

14. *Oratio contra gentes,* 41, MPG 25, 81-84. See the comments on the relation between grace and creation in J. B. Berchem, "Le rôle du Verbe dans l'oeuvre de la création et de la sanctification d'après saint Athanase," *Angelicum,* XV (1938), 201-232.

15. *Oratio de incarnatione Verbi,* 43, MPG 25, 172.

16. *Oratio contra gentes,* 40, MPG 25, 81.

17. *Orationes contra Arianos*, II, 10, *MPG* 26, 165.
18. *Vita Sancti Antonii*, 76, *MPG* 26, 949.
19. *Ibid.*, 24, *MPG* 26, 880. The brief notes of Father Daniélou on the demonology of the *Life of Saint Antony* are quite suggestive: Jean Daniélou, "Les démons de l'air dans la 'Vie d'Antoine,'" *Studia Anselmiana*, XXXVIII (1956), 136-145.
20. *Orationes contra Arianos*, II, 43, *MPG* 26, 237.
21. See, for example, Arnobius, *Adversus nationes*, V, 30.
22. *Oratio contra gentes*, 29, *MPG* 25, 57.
23. *Ibid.*, 38, *MPG* 25, 76.
24. *Orationes contra Arianos*, III, 15-16, *MPG* 26, 352-357.
25. *Ibid.*, 8, *MPG* 26, 336-337.
26. *Orationes contra Arianos*, II, 32, *MPG* 26, 216.
27. *Oratio de incarnatione Verbi*, 12, *MPG* 25, 117.
28. *Oratio contra gentes*, 38, *MPG* 25, 76-77.
29. *Ibid.*, 45, *MPG* 25, 89.
30. *Ad episcopos Aegypti* (written in A.D. 356-357), 15, *MPG* 25, 572-573. The verb translated as "infer" both in this passage and in the passage from the *Oratio contra gentes* referred to in note 29 is *enthymeomai*.

3 THE RADIANCE OF THE FATHER

1. Jaroslav Pelikan, *Luther the Expositor*, pp. 14-18. The exegesis of Proverbs 8 occupies the bulk of Athanasius' *Second Discourse against the Arians, Orationes contra Arianos*, II, 18-82, *MPG* 26, 184-321; for other instances, cf. Müller, *op. cit.*, col. 1641.
2. Father Daniélou's *Sacramentum futuri*, now translated into English, summarizes much of the exegesis of these centuries: Jean Daniélou, *From Shadows to Reality. Studies in the Biblical Typology of the Fathers*, trans. Wulstan Hibberd (Westminster, Md., 1960). J. Rendel Harris, *Testimonies* (Cambridge, 1916) enumerates many of the passages that figured in this exegesis. Cf. also Joseph P. Smith, "Introduction" to Irenaeus, *Proof of the Apostolic Preaching*, No. 16 of "Ancient Christian Writers" (Westminster, Md., 1952), pp. 31 ff.
3. G. L. Prestige, *God in Patristic Thought*, p. 298.
4. See Gerhard Kittel *s.v.* "apaugasma" in Gerhard Kittel (ed.), *Theologisches Wörterbuch zum Neuen Testament*, I (Stuttgart, 1933), 505, on the backgrounds of the term in the Septuagint and in Philo; also Ceslaus Spicq, *L'epitre aux Hébreux* (Paris, 1952-1953), II, 6-7 on the active and passive interpretations of *apaugasma*, with both Philonic and patristic references.
5. Justin, *Dialogus cum Tryphone Judaeo*, 61; Tatian, *Oratio ad Graecos*, 5.
6. *De decretis Nicaenae synodi*, 23, *MPG* 25, 456.
7. Cf. Hans-Georg Opitz, "Dionys von Alexandrien und die Libyer" in Robert P. Casey (ed.), *Studies Presented to Kirsopp Lake* (London, 1937), pp. 41-53.

8. *De sententia Dionysii, MPG* 25, 479.

9. *Ibid.*, 15, *MPG* 25, 501.

10. *De decretis Nicaenae synodi*, 27, *MPG* 25, 465.

11. *Ibid.*, 25, *MPG* 25, 460.

12. Tertullian, *Apologeticus*, 21.

13. Cf. Jaroslav Pelikan, "Montanism and Its Trinitarian Significance," *Church History*, XXV-2 (June, 1956), 99-109, esp. 106-107.

14. On the history of the term *probolē*, see the note of Ernest Evans, *Tertullian's Treatise Against Praxeas*, pp. 239-240.

15. Adolf Harnack, *Outlines of the History of Dogma*, trans. Edwin Knox Mitchell (Boston, 1957), p. 242.

16. See p. 22 above.

17. Cf. *De synodis*, 42, *MPG* 26, 768. On the charge that the orthodox doctrine introduced carnal thought and language into religion, cf. Johann Adam Möhler, *Athanasius der Grosse und die Kirche seiner Zeit* (Mainz, 1827), I, 271-276.

18. Therefore the pseudo-Athanasian *Fourth Discourse against the Arians* correctly saw in the image "Son of God" the way to refute Sabellianism. *Orationes contra Arianos*, IV, 3, *MPG* 26, 472. In general, see T. E. Pollard, "Logos and Son in Origen, Arius and Athanasius," *Studia Patristica*, II (Berlin, 1957) 282-287.

19. *Orationes contra Arianos*, I, 9, *MPG* 26, 28-29.

20. *Ibid.*, II, 2, *MPG* 26, 149.

21. *Ibid.*, I, 24, *MPG* 26, 61. On the background of this pun, cf. V. Rose, "Question johannine. Les Aloges asiatiques et les aloges romains," *Revue biblique*, VI (1897), 516-534.

22. See p. 48, note 24 above; also G. L. Prestige, *Fathers and Heretics* (London, 1948), pp. 67-93.

23. *Orationes contra Arianos*, I, 13, *MPG* 26, 40.

24. *Ibid.*, III, 66, *MPG* 26, 464. On the controversy over the idea that the Son had come into existence by the will of the Father, cf. Ferdinand Cavallera, *Saint Athanase* (Paris, 1908), pp. 82-85.

25. *Orationes contra Arianos*, I, 16, *MPG* 26, 45.

26. *Ibid.*, III, 36, *MPG* 26, 401.

27. *Ibid.*, I, 25, *MPG* 26, 64.

28. On the history of the term, cf. Prestige, *God in Patristic Thought*, pp. 197-218.

29. *De decretis Nicaenae synodi*, 24, *MPG* 25, 457.

30. *Ibid.* See the similar argument in *Orationes contra Arianos*, I, 25, *MPG* 26, 64.

31. *Epistola ad Afros*, 8, *MPG* 26, 1044.

32. See pp. 34-36 above.

33. *Orationes contra Arianos*, II, 33, *MPG* 26, 217.

34. *De sententia Dionysii*, 24, *MPG* 25, 516.

35. *In illud*, "Omnia mihi tradita etc.," 4, *MPG* 25, 216.

36. *Epistola ad episcopos Aegypti*, 13, *MPG* 25, 568.

37. *De synodis*, 16, *MPG* 26, 709. Cf. the comments of J. Lebon, "Le

sort de consubstantiel nicéen," *Revue historique*, XLVII (1952), 485-529.

38. Eduard Schwartz points out that "there was in existence no orthodox interpretation of *homoousia*, which could be set into opposition with the Oriental [interpretation], drawn from Origen; and, to say the least, Athanasius had an advantage in creating" such an interpretation. *Zur Geschichte des Athanasius, Gesammelte Schriften*, III (Berlin, 1959), 318.

39. *De synodis*, 52, *MPG* 26, 788.

40. *Orationes contra Arianos*, III, 4, *MPG* 26, 329.

41. *Ibid.*, III, 13, *MPG* 26, 349.

42. *Oratio contra gentes*, 46, *MPG* 25, 93. The term *autophōs*, which Athanasius employs here as part of a rhetorical catena—*autosophia, autologos, autodynamis, autophōs, autoalētheia, autodikaiosynē, autoaretē*—occurs nowhere else in his works. It does, however, appear (together with *autozōē*) in Eusebius, *Demonstratio evangelica*, IV, 13.

43. *Oratio de incarnatione Verbi*, 17, *MPG* 25, 125.

44. The adequacy of Athanasius' Christology and its relation to later Christological thought, especially to Apollinarianism, have been the subject of considerable controversy. The Protestant scholar Alfred Stülcken in *Athanasiana*, "Texte und Untersuchungen," IV-4 (Leipzig, 1899), pp. 81-150, questioned Athanasius' doctrine of the humanity of Christ. The Roman Catholic scholar Eduard Weigl in *Untersuchungen zur Christologie des heiligen Athanasius*, "Forschungen zur christlichen Literatur- und Dogmengeschichte," XII-4 (Paderborn, 1914), attempted, on both theological and literary grounds, to exoneratae Athanasius. It would seem that the controversy has been settled by the masterful researches of another Roman Catholic theologian, Aloys Grillmeier, in "Die theologische und sprachliche Vorbereitung der christologischen Formel von Chalkedon," in Aloys Grillmeier and Heinrich Bacht (eds.), *Das Konzil von Chalkedon* (Würzburg, 1951), I, 5-202; on Athanasius see 77-102. But Grillmeier's thesis is still being debated.

45. *Epistolae ad Serapionem*, I, 19-20, *MPG* 26, 573-577.

46. Cf. Prestige, *God in Patristic Thought*, pp. 282-300.

4 SALVATION AS ILLUMINATION

1. *Sermo major de fide*, 22, *MPG* 26, 1276. On the basis of an Armenian manuscript, Robert P. Casey concludes that the *Sermo* was "originally a letter addressed to the church at Antioch." Cf. his brief note, "The pseudo-Athanasian Sermo maior de fide," *Journal of Theological Studies*, XXXV (1934), 394.

2. On the importance of the *Life of St. Antony*, cf. Karl Heussi, *Der Ursprung des Mönchtums* (Tübingen, 1936), pp. 78-108.

3. *Vita S. Antonii*, 10, *MPG* 26, 860.

4. See pp. 42-44.

5. Cf. Friedrich Hauck, *Das Evangelium des Lukas*, "Theologisches

Handkommentar zum Neuen Testament," III (Leipzig, 1934), 114; also W. Heitmüller, *Im Namen Jesu* (Göttingen, 1903), esp. p. 250 ff., and Origen, *Contra Celsum*, I, 6.

6. Edward Gibbon, *The Decline and Fall of the Roman Empire*, Chap. XXI.

7. Adolf Harnack, *Lehrbuch der Dogmengeschichte* (5th ed.; Tübingen, 1931), II, 208-209.

8. See the comments of Karl Barth, *Kirchliche Dogmatik*, III-2 (Zürich, 1948), 71-72; and those of Dietrich Bonhoeffer, "Christologie," *Gesammelte Schriften* ed. Eberhard Bethge, III (München, 1960), 176-178.

9. *In illud, "Omnia mihi tradita etc.,"* 2, *MPG* 25, 212.

10. *Orationes contra Arianos*, III, 35, *MPG* 26, 400.

11. *Ibid.*, I, 47, *MPG* 26, 109.

12. *Ibid.*, I, 24, *MPG* 26, 61.

13. Cf. J. B. Berchem, "Le rôle du Verbe dans l'oeuvre de la création et de la sanctification d'après saint Athanase," *Angelicum*, XV (1938), 201-232.

14. *Oratio contra gentes*, 1, *MPG* 25, 5.

15. *Oratio de incarnatione Verbi*, 32, *MPG* 25, 152.

16. See pp. 103-107.

17. *Oratio de incarnatione Verbi*, 17, *MPG* 25, 125; on the problems created by this terminology, cf. Louis Coulange, "Métamorphose du consubstantiel: Athanase et Hilaire," *Revue d'histoire et de litterature religieuses* (Nouvelle Serie), VIII (1922), 169-214, esp. 169-186, 207-214.

18. Cf. Harnack, *Lehrbuch*, II, 46-47, for a catalogue of Greek fathers on deification.

19. *Oratio de incarnatione Verbi*, 54, *MPG* 25, 192; see the sober discussions of K. Bornhäuser, *Die Vergottungslehre des Athanasius und Johannes Damascenus* (Gütersloh, 1903), pp. 13-48, and of J. Gross, *La divinisation du chrétien d'après les pères grecs* (Paris, 1938), pp. 201-218.

20. See Ernst Wolf, "Asterisci und Obelisci zum Thema: Athanasius und Luther," *Evangelische Theologie*, XVIII (1958), 481-490, which is an effort to subordinate "deification" and "incarnation-theology" to a radical theology of the Word of God. Also Regin Prenter, *Schöpfung und Erlösung. Dogmatik*, II (Göttingen, 1960), 347-380, which seeks to draw Luther and Athanasius closer together.

21. Perhaps the most complete exposition is in *Orationes contra Arianos*, III, 19-23, *MPG* 26, 361-372.

22. *Oratio de incarnatione Verbi*, 55, *MPG* 25, 193.

23. *Oratio contra gentes*, 23, *MPG* 25, 48.

24. *Vita S. Antonii*, 79, *MPG* 26, 953.

25. *Orationes contra Arianos*, I, 16, *MPG* 26, 45, quoting 2 Peter 1:4.

26. *Orationes contra Arianos*, I, 43, *MPG* 26, 100-101.

27. *Ibid.*, III, 24, *MPG* 26, 373.

28. *Ibid.*, III, 10, *MPG* 26, 341; on this entire problem see R. Bernard, *L'image de Dieu d'après saint Athanase* (Paris, 1952).

29. *Orationes contra Arianos*, II, 76, *MPG* 26, 308.

30. *Epistola ad episcopos Aegypti*, 18, MPG 25, 580.
31. *Oratio de incarnatione Verbi*, 40, MPG 25, 168.
32. Justin, *Apologia* I, 65.
33. *Epistolae ad Serapionem*, I, 6, MPG 26, 544.
34. *Orationes contra Arianos*, I, 48, MPG 26, 112-113.
35. *Ibid.*, II, 41, MPG 26, 233. As G. W. H. Lampe has said, "there is an urgent need for a full and impartial investigation of the real teaching of the fathers on baptism and the gift of the Spirit," *The Seal of the Spirit* (London, 1951), p. 195.
36. *Oratio contra gentes*, 27, MPG 25, 53. Cf. also the probably pseudonymous *De virginitate*, 25, MPG 28, 281.
37. *Oratio contra gentes*, 7, MPG 25, 16.
38. *Ibid.*, 1, MPG 25, 5.
39. F. L. Cross, *The Study of St. Athanasius* (Oxford, 1945), p. 5.

5 CHILDREN OF THE LIGHT

1. *Orationes contra Arianos*, IV, 18, MPG 26, 493.
2. *Epistolae ad Serapionem*, I, 19, MPG 26, 573.
3. For a summary of Athanasius' controversies on the coequality of the Holy Spirit, cf. Theodor Schermann, *Die Gottheit des Heiligen Geistes nach den griechischen Vätern des vierten Jahrhunderts* (Freiburg, 1901), pp. 47-89; also Joseph Lebon, "Introduction" to Athanasius' *Lettres à Sérapion sur la divinité du Saint-Esprit* ("Sources chrétiennes," 15; Paris, 1947), pp. 52-77.
4. *Orationes contra Arianos*, I, 43, MPG 26, 101.
5. *Apologia de fuga sua*, 13, MPG 25, 661. Cf. Gustave Bardy, *Saint Athanase* (2nd ed.; Paris, 1914), pp. 140-142.
6. *Orationes contra Arianos*, II, 64, MPG 26, 284.
7. Cf. H. Richard Niebuhr, *The Kingdom of God in America* (New York, 1937), pp. 19-21.
8. *Oratio de incarnatione Verbi*, 57, MPG 25, 196-197.
9. Cf. Gustave Bardy, "La vie spirituelle d'après saint Athanase," *La vie spirituelle*, XVIII (1928), 97-113.
10. *Vita S. Antonii*, 94, MPG 26, 976.
11. *Ibid.*, 14, MPG 26, 864-865.
12. *Ibid.*, 84, MPG 26, 961.
13. *Ibid.*, 81, MPG 26, 956-957; see the summary discussion of Karl Friedrich Hagel, *Kirche und Kaisertum in Lehre und Leben des Athanasius* (Leipzig, 1933), pp. 70-76.
14. There is a careful examination of the terminology in Athanasius' *Life of St. Antony* by Basilius Steidle, "Homo Dei Antonius. Zum Bild des 'Mannes Gottes' im alten Mönchtum," *Studia Anselmiana*, XXXVIII (1956), 148-200; see especially 176-183. This entire volume of the *Studia Anselmiana* is helpful in the study of the *Life*.
15. *Vita S. Antonii*, 61, MPG 26, 932.
16. *Ibid.*, 67, MPG 26, 940.

17. Robert T. Meyer, "Notes" to St. Athanasius, *The Life of St. Antony*, No. 10 of "Ancient Christian Writers" (Westminster, Md., 1950), p. 126, note 227, with parallels.

18. *Vita S. Antonii*, 42, MPG 26, 905.

19. *Oratio contra gentes*, 3, MPG 25, 8-9.

20. On the earlier backgrounds of this, cf. Jaroslav Pelikan, *The Shape of Death* (New York, 1961), especially the discussion of Irenaeus, with whom Athanasius' view of death displayed many affinities.

21. Cf. *Vita S. Antonii*, 46-47, MPG 26, 909-912 on martyrdom and monasticism; also Edward E. Malone, "The Monk and the Martyr," *Studia Anselmiana*, XXXVIII (1956), 212-218.

22. *Oratio de incarnatione Verbi*, 27-28, MPG 25, 141-145.

23. *Vita S. Antonii*, 19, MPG 26, 872.

24. *Oratio de incarnatione Verbi*, 29, MPG 25, 145.

25. *Ibid.*, 32, MPG 25, 152.

26. *Vita S. Antonii*, 35, MPG 26, 896. See the interesting comment on this passage in Kenneth E. Kirk, *The Vision of God* (2nd ed.; London, 1932), pp. 181-184.

27. *Vita S. Antonii*, 93, MPG 26, 973.

28. *Epistolae ad Serapionem*, I, 12, MPG 26, 561.

29. Cf. Paul S. Minear, *Images of the Church in the New Testament*, pp. 127-129.

30. *Vita S. Antonii*, 69, MPG 26, 941.

31. *Oratio de incarnatione Verbi*, 24, MPG 25, 137; cf. Louis Bouyer, *L'Incarnation et l'Église-corps du Christ dans la théologie de saint Athanase* (Paris, 1943), pp. 85-90 on the doctrine of the church in the *Oratio de incarnatione Verbi*.

INDEXES

Ancient Authors

Modern Authors

Biblical References

Greek Terms Cited or Explained
(arranged according to the Greek alphabet)

DATE DUE